Tupelo Press Poetry in Translation: Previous Volumes

Abiding Places: Korea, South and North, by Ko Un
   Translated from Korean by Hillel Schwartz and Sunny Jung

Invitation to a Secret Feast: Selected Poems, by Joumana Haddad
   Translated from Arabic by Khaled Mattawa with the poet, and with Najib Awad, Issa Boullata, Marilyn Hacker, Henry Matthews, and David Harsent

Night, Fish and Charlie Parker, by Phan Nhien Hao
   Translated from Vietnamese by Linh Dinh

Stone Lyre: Poems of René Char
   Translated from French by Nancy Naomi Carlson

This Lamentable City: Poems of Polina Barskova
   Edited by Ilya Kaminsky and translated from Russian by the editor with the poet, and with Katie Farris, Rachel Galvin, and Matthew Zapruder

New Cathay: Contemporary Chinese Poetry
   Edited by Ming Di and translated from Chinese by the editor with Neil Aitken, Katie Farris, Christopher Lupke, Tony Barnstone, Nick Admussen, Jonathan Stalling, Afaa M. Weaver, Eleanor Goodman, Ao Wang, Dian Li, Kerry Shawn Keys, Jennifer Kronovet, Elizabeth Reitzell, and Cody Reese

Ex-Voto, by Adélia Prado
   Translated from Brazilian Portuguese by Ellen Doré Watson with the poet

Gossip and Metaphysics: Russian Modernist Poems and Prose
   Edited by Katie Farris, Ilya Kaminsky, and Valzhyna Mort, with translations by the editors and others

Calazaza's Delicious Dereliction, by Suzanne Dracius
   Translated from French by Nancy Naomi Carlson with the poet

Canto General: Song of the Americas, by Pablo Neruda
   Translated from Spanish by Mariela Griffor and Jeffrey Levine

Hammer with No Master, by René Char
   Translated from French by Nancy Naomi Carlson

A Certain Roughness in Their Syntax, by Jorge Aulicino
   Translated from Spanish by Judith Filc with the poet

xeixa

FOURTEEN CATALAN POETS

Edited and translated from Catalan
by Marlon L. Fick and Francisca Esteve

T|P

TUPELO PRESS
North Adams, Massachusetts

Xeixa: Fourteen Catalan Poets.
Translation from Catalan. selection, and introduction copyright © 2018 Marlon Fick and
Francisca Esteve. All rights reserved.

Library of Congress Cataloging-in-Publication Data
Names: Fick, Marlon L., 1960– editor, translator. | Esteve, Francisca,
 editor, translator.
Title: Xeixa : fourteen Catalan poets / edited and translated from Catalan by
 Marlon L. Fick and Francisca Esteve.
Other titles: Tupelo Press poetry in translation.
Description: First paperback edition. | North Adams, Massachusetts : Tupelo
 Press, [2018] | Series: Tupelo Press poetry in translation | Includes
 bibliographical references.
Identifiers: LCCN 2018043424 | ISBN 9781946482167 (pbk. original : alk. paper)
Subjects: LCSH: Catalan poetry—Translations into English.
Classification: LCC PC3929 .X45 2018 | DDC 849/.91608--dc23

Cover and text designed and composed in Mrs Eaves and Helvetica by Howard Klein.

Cover art: Albert Ràfols-Casamada (1923–2009), Deep Blue (1959). Oil on canvas, 146 x 114
cm. Copyright © 2018 Artists Rights Society (ARS), New York / VEGAP, Madrid. Used with
permission. Photo: Martí Gasull, courtesy Art Resource, NY.

First paperback edition: November 2018.

Tupelo Press
P.O. Box 1767, North Adams, Massachusetts 01247
(413) 664-9611 / editor@tupelopress.org / www.tupelopress.org

Tupelo Press is an award-winning independent literary press that publishes fine fiction,
nonfiction, and poetry in books that are a joy to hold as well as read. Tupelo Press is a
registered 501(c)(3) nonprofit organization, and we rely on public support to carry out
our mission of publishing extraordinary work that may be outside the realm of the large
commercial publishers. Financial donations are welcome and are tax deductible.

The translation of this work has been supported by the Institut Ramon Llull, with publication
also supported in part by an award from the National Endowment for the Arts

LLLL institut
ramon llull
Catalan Language and Culture

ART WORKS.
arts.gov

Contents

David Castillo

Translating Catalan Poetry

In the autumn of 2015, editor Jeffrey Levine at Tupelo Press suggested
that my wife Francisca Esteve and I collaborate in curating and translating
an anthology of Catalan poetry, child of Provençal. My activities as a
translator have principally been in Spanish and French, with forays
into German and Chinese. On the other hand, Francisca is a native
speaker of Catalan. She came of age in the time of the dictator General
Francisco Franco, and along with nine million other speakers of Catalan,
she suffered from laws forbidding her language. In the 1960s and '70s,
Francisca met regularly (at the same Barcelona café frequented in the
1930s by George Orwell, near the Plaza del Pi) with her friends in the
anti-fascist underground, talking strategy and planning ways to subvert
the Franco government. If you were lucky, overheard speaking Catalan,
a *Tricornio* (the police with three-cornered hats) would shake a finger
and shout, "Speak Christian!" (meaning Castilian Spanish); if unlucky,
prison. Her job was to smuggle and disseminate books and pamphlets
in the Catalan language. During this time, many "disappeared." No
one is certain about the post-war casualties, but some have estimated the
number at over a million during Franco's forty years of repression.

Despite Franco, the language and culture has been surprisingly resilient
over the past thousand years. In this anthology, *Catalunya* (the Catalan
spelling of Catalonia) refers to the four Spanish provinces of Barcelona,
Girona, Lleida, and Tarragona, and also to Valencia and its three
provinces in the south, the Balearic Islands (Mallorca, Menorca, Ibiza,
and Formentera) in the western Mediterranean Sea, and Andorra to the
north. Yet *Catalunya* is more than a geographical region; Catalan implies a
culture and sensibility, not only a language or political entity.
The Greeks established a trade colony in the vicinity of modern-day

Gerona, called Ampurias, in 575 BCE. In 318 BCE, the Romans used what is present-day *Catalunya* as their point of entry to invade and occupy the entire peninsula, establishing Latin as the primary language. In the fifth and sixth centuries, the Visigoths invaded the region. By the eighth century, the entire peninsula was controlled by the Moors, which is why one can find a great many Arabic words in both Catalan and Spanish. When the Moors tried to expand into France, Charles Martel defeated them at the Battle of Tours (732 CE). Later, his grandson Charlemagne pushed them back again, using the Pyrenees as a wall between the two empires.

Catalan culture as we know it today begins to take shape in the twelfth century. In 1137, when Count Ramon Berenger IV of *Catalunya* wed Princess Petronilla of Aragon, both regions continued their own administrative policies and languages. Their union resulted in further expansion of *Catalunya* and the Catalan language, to the North and South, to Valencia, the Balaeric Islands, and Andorra—regions of Catalan language and culture now under Castilian domain.

Practically speaking, *Catalunya* has been distinct from Spain for most of the past thousand years, with some interruptions. Over the next three hundred years, Catalan areas (such as Valencia and the Balearic Islands) fell to Spain, but even then, the Catalan language and culture continued. During the High Renaissance, Rome even saw the rise of a Catalan Pope, Alexander VI, a Borgia who spoke and wrote in Catalan, although he was referred to as "The Spanish Pope." However, Spain did continue its dominance. As Franco would later do, the eighteenth-century Bourbon king Felipe V forbade the speaking of Catalan after winning the War of the Spanish Succession (1701–13), wresting away power from the Austrian Habsburg Dynasty, to whom *Catalunya* had lent support. (Words from the German language appear in Catalan as a result of this alliance.) But Catalan survived. The industrial revolutions of 1840 and 1891 were

Catalan peasant rebellions against the exploitation of their labor. 1880 was a year that marked a cultural renaissance for *Catalunya*, in writing and in the arts. And 1873 saw the first intent to establish a sovereign government.

The pre–Civil War Constitution of 1931 echoed *Catalunya*'s traditional independence, with a spirit in keeping with centuries.

After the death of Franco, autonomy again returned to the region. Spain's Constitution of 1978, however, contained a vaguely worded clause (article 144) that stipulated the Catalan provinces would remain part of Spain. Now governed only semi-autonomously, many Catalans complain that Madrid exacts taxes that are unfair, far in excess of what the rest of Spain pays. Whether perception or reality, heavy taxation has fanned the flames of separatism in Caluyna. The October 1, 2017, referendum on independence was ruled illegal by Madrid, and President Puigdemont of *Catalunya* was arrested.

Through these age-old conflicts and historic upheavals, the Catalan language has survived. Barcelona, capital of *Catalunya*, now flourishes with numerous publishing houses dedicated to Catalan literature in all of its regions.

Catalan developed around the same time as the other Romance languages— French, Italian—in the twelfth and thirteenth centuries, coinciding with the Anglo Saxon and French-Latin hybrid that is English during the time of Chaucer. In many respects, Catalan poetry is the child of Provençal. The mystical and passionate poet, Ramon Llull (c. 1232 – c. 1315), author of *Llibre D'Amic i Amat (The Book of Love and the Beloved)*, was the first great Catalan master. A poet of his magnitude is a necessary condition for a language to fully bloom. English had Shakespeare; Russian, Tolstoy; Spanish, Cervantes. Catalan is not a dialect of Spanish. It is its own language. One only need glance at a page to recognize its status as a romance language beyond the definition of a dialect.

The following is the original version of a poem by Joan Margarit that appears in this anthology:

Al Fons de la Nit

Está glaçant a l'aire.
Ha callat fins i tot el rossinyol.
Amb el front recolzat damunt del vidre
demano que em perdonin
les meves dues filles mortes
perquè ja gairebé no penso en elles.
El temps ha anat deixant argila seca
damunt la cicatriu. I, fins i tot
quan un s'estima algú, arriba l'oblit.
La llum té la duresa de les gotes
que cauen dels xiprers amb el desgel.
Poso un tronc nou i, removent les cendres,
trec flama de les brases. Faig cafè.
La vostra mare surt del dormitori
amb un somriure: *Quina bona olor.*
T'has aixecat molt d'hora aquest matí.

The title itself is closer to French than Spanish: "Au fond de la nuit," not "En lo hondo de la noche." A reader familiar with the poetry of François Villon or later French poets will find at least a dozen French cognates per page. Likewise, readers familiar with Dante's Italian will find a dozen cognates. Catalan's vocabulary does share commonalities with

Spanish, of course, but the majority of Catalan words do not come from Spanish; like other romance languages, Catalan comes from Latin.

The task of translating in the shadow of Catalan's rich past is daunting and humbling. Since my wife is a natural speaker, however, and since my Spanish and French are strong and my training is in the history of poetics, we agreed to take up Tupelo Press on the challenge. In May of 2016 we traveled to Catalonia and Valencia to meet with a number of poets, among them Joan Margarit, Màrius Sampere, David Castillo, Jordi Valls, Josep Piera, Francesc Parcerisas, Manuel Forcano, Antoni Marí, and Feliu Formosa. Others we reached by mail: Teresa Pascual, Ponç Pons, Cèlia Sànchez-Mústich, Laia Noguera, Anna Gual, Jordi Virallonga, Àngels Gregori i Parra, Rosa Font, and Antònia Vicens. Long, intense, and delightful conversations ensued.

For example, one day Josep Piera met us at the train station of Gandia, Valencia, around 11:00 a.m. We began talking (about history, poetry, poetic movements, the history of Valencia, politics, paella ...) and before any of us realized, it was suddenly three o'clock in the morning! Similarly, Jordi Valls met us on several occasions at Bracafé by the Plaza Catalunya in Barcelona, thereupon taking us on long walking tours of the city, teaching us peripatetically the interrelations of art, architecture, history, and poetry. Others, like Antoni Marí, graciously filled us in on Petrarch's contributions to Catalan literature. Joan Margarit and I exchanged our views on poets and translations. We received from Margarit and Sampere and Parcerisas extremely good advice on what sort of direction our anthology should take. But it was Carmen Sampere, Màrius's wife, who helped us contact the important women writing in Catalan. Sampere's generation (he was born in 1928) tended to dismiss talented women, owing to a culture of machismo, although he himself shows no signs of such bias. The fact remains that the women poets born in the 1930s through the '50s were often invisible. We are including a number of women poets here not to fill an obligatory quota, but because it is justice that they now take their place beside the men.

Before long, we had received as gifts hundreds of books to survey, in addition to the hundreds we purchased ourselves. The most common question a poet or potential reader would ask is, "What is your criteria for selection?" All of the aforementioned poets have already established their fame at home, and many of them are known internationally. Yet I am less interested in accolades than the poem I see on a page. There are many brilliant poets in the Catalan language, but sometimes the field of reference is so local that translating would entail a long list of explanatory footnotes, and the poem would be lost in translation.

Early in the process, Francisca and I decided we would only translate poems that both of us liked, whether the enjoyment grew from the richness of the language or from a particular theme. As a reader, I want to be moved. In addition, my wife's background is in painting, not poetry. To be sure, she is smart, but this anthology represents her first introduction to the world of translating poetry, in any language. So I've relied on her freshness. If an intelligent reader, not academically trained in poetry, is moved by a poem, I sit up and take notice. My own half-century of involvement in poetry may be valuable, but I cannot claim to see poetry "for the first time." This is an element of magic that I decided we could make essential to our process. One day, she emerged from her office in a state of childlike joy and amazement, clutching a volume by Sampere, exclaiming, "Sampere wrote a poem about stoplights that you have to read!"

Regarding our method, Francisca first reads and glosses the poetry, often tracking down dialect differences between Catalan in Catalonia or in Valencia or Mallorca. She is usually aware of the differences without a dictionary since she was born in Castellón de Rugat, Valencia. Her parents took her to Barcelona when she was three months old, but her mother Valenciana continued to speak Catalan from her native region. Francisca's teachers, who were nuns, were all from Mallorca. So she has a grasp of all three dominant dialects of Catalan. When we encounter dialect differences, in the poetry of Pons (Menorcan) and Piera (Valenciano), Francisca hears her mother's voice again or the voices of the Sisters. Indeed, the differences within Catalan are sometimes radical: For instance, the word for "sunset" is *capvespre* in Catalonia, *vesprada* in Valencia, and *horabaixa* in the five Balearic Islands.

Our translation method is consistent: We both study the poem in Catalan. We discuss the poem in Spanish and in English. She tells me her version of the poem, and I write my version in English. Then I read back my version to her, verbally translating my English into Spanish as she carefully follows the original text in Catalan. This is a process known as "back translation," a technique conceived of by Saint Jerome, the man responsible for translating the Vulgate Latin Bible in the fourth century. In this way, we are confident that we have ensured fidelity. However, we do not end there. Once we are confident, we send our version back to the poet, some of whom do know English (Parcerisas, for instance, is famous for his translations of English poetry). The poets who do not know English share our translations with a trusted friend and then formally approve, or in some cases suggest changes.

Translators routinely experience frustration when encountering impossible, beautifully lyrical lines that repeat a word with multiple uses. Josep Piera writes "*I vol la veu que veu al vol,*" which, sadly, becomes "and the voice wants to see flight," a line without its original chiasmus, since there are no English words that double their signification the same way.

Similarly, he writes, "*Cau la nit com un cau*," again translated without its original sonic breadth: "Night falls like a lair."

In reading and conversations, we learned that Catalan poetry is dominantly a literature of lyric tradition. Most poems do not attempt to tell a story; the existence of some narrative poetry in Catalan is a borrowing from the English and American traditions. The chief external influence on Catalan poetry comes from the French tradition; in particular, from the Symbolist movement. Catalan poets are profoundly familiar with the lineage of Baudelaire, Verlaine, Rimbaud, and Laforgue. A symbol, by its very essence, is a centrifugal force of meaning, spinning just beyond our grasp. Just so, the Symbolist may write lines that extend beyond the edges of clarity to a zone between the world of reference and the beyond. The influence of the Symbolists affected Catalan poets as much the British and Americans—notably W. B. Yeats and T. S. Eliot.

While the influence of the French Symbolists has not dissipated even now, a second influence emerged in Catalan letters after the death of Franco: the American "Beat generation." In the summer of 2016, both the Pompidou in Paris and the Contemporary Art Museum of Barcelona held special exhibitions dedicated to the Beats. Burroughs, Ginsberg, and Kerouac are idolized among some of the younger poets, who have only recently discovered them. The attraction is understandable, given Spain's history. Spanish anarchism predates the worldwide rebellion against authoritarianism, beginning before World War I and the dying gasp of monarchical rule. In other words, Beat poets and hippies did not invent social and literary revolution. We are not suggesting that Spain is unique in its political and artistic revolt. The Romantics pushed against the edges of acceptability at every turn, from social mores to epistemology. More recently, by the 1920s André Breton and Gertrude Stein were promoting revolution on a syntactical and grammatical level. They believed that grammar—and its cousin punctuation—were the tools of patriarchal tyranny, a tyranny that had seeped into the unconscious, and the only way to purge the mind of oppression was to dismantle language structures, eradicate punctuation, and hack away at syntax as one might dismember an enemy. The notion of properly punctuating a sentence or a line of poetry as a courtesy to a reader so that he or she might follow the drift took second place to a poetic exploration of what might lie beyond the edges of sensibility. The Catalan poets participated in this rebellion as much as any other group. Josep Piera, for instance, rarely punctuates. What he does instead is rely on the white space, which some may call silence, to carry the reader. Indeed, through all their experimentation, Piera and Castillo—from the older and younger generations, respectively—have both proven to be immensely talented.

Although individual poets in this anthology differ in their aesthetics, there is a little anecdote that may serve to illustrate just how unified Catalan poets are. I overheard a young American in Barcelona's gothic neighborhood ask his tour guide: "With all these cathedrals, the Catalan people must be a very religious!" Her reply was, "Not so much." Indeed, virtually all of these poets question the existence of God and express, usually in irony, an agnostic or perhaps even atheistic point of view. Catalan poets rebel against the theological tyranny that, for centuries, was forced on them by the Holy Roman Church. Pope Pius XII sided with Franco and the Fascists, not the Republicans. So, while there may be differences among contemporary Catalan poets regarding the degree to which their poems lean toward or away from sense, there is collective agreement that existence precedes essence. Readers may remember T. S. Eliot's critique of Baudelaire, in which Eliot distinguishes "high blasphemy" from "low." There is a grittiness about the Catalan poets that trumps lofty philosophy and theology. And while their commentaries on metaphysical matters may be sarcastic, they are nevertheless high-minded.

Stylistically, Teresa Pascual, David Castillo, Jordi Valls, Cèlia Sànchez-Mústich, and Josep Piera write poetry that is beautiful and dense. Others—Joan Margarit, Màrius Sampere, Antònia Vicens, Francesc Parcerisas, Jordi Virallonga, Ponç Pons—write poetry with clarity and precision. Margarit seems to have no patience for poetry that evades coherence. In "Reading Poetry," he writes: "When I finish this book of poems / by Paul Celan, I know neither / what he said / nor what he wanted to tell me. I don't even know / if he were pretending to tell me something. / Hermetic poets are terrified." Margarit's poetry is tethered to this world, providing awareness of complex moods. Even when he meditates on symbolism in Baudelaire, we still know exactly where and when this occurs. The most ephemeral thought in a poem by Margarit is anchored to a place or a memory and the objects around him.

Likewise, Sampere grants his readers the relief that comes from clarity. At the same time, his vision is unlike any other. His greatest gift is the ability to surprise us in every poem. No one can predict what he will say or write. He is a magician among poets, so sleight-of-hand that we will never grasp the secrets behind his curtain. If, in translating, we have given Margarit and Sampere more pages than others, it is because we are transfixed by their genius, and we wish our readers to understand why. It is no wonder that both of them have been short-listed for the Nobel Prize.

Regarding their generation—Margarit is eighty and Sampere is ninety—we will acknowledge again a regret we share with many: publishers and critics have paid more attention to men than to women. The women began to emerge later. Theirs is a poetry of densely taut centers of psychological and emotional awareness. Teresa Pascual, Cèlia Sànchez-Mústich, Rosa

Font, and Antònia Vicens are giants. Vicens's poem "The Ways" is written in long lines in a series of parentheses, as if to say that a woman might comment on her repression should she be allowed to do so. Vicens, Pascual, Sànchez-Mústich, and Font write poems that are fully realized in both form and content. They are masters of technique who never become so obscure as to cause their readers to feel lost.

Today there are thousands of poets writing in Catalan. Ultimately, our goal with this anthology was not to be encyclopedic but rather to focus on and celebrate men and women whose work has reached maturity, and to extend to them an international renown, so long delayed by fascism. In the end, there are fourteen poets featured here, nine more than we had anticipated.

Finally, a note about our title. *Xeixa* (pronounced *zhay-zha*) is one of the first words I learned in Catalan, and I think it is exquisite. It is the word for a rare and very high-quality type of wheat, as such symbolic of beauty, plentitude, bounty, sustenance, grace, and the rarity of genius that readers will find and reap from these pages.

—Marlon L. Fick

STILL A PROLOGUE

Time has passed.

Time was born there.
It cried from the branches,
pulled from the seeds.
Time was utterly
an embrace from inside.
And the moon, pushing aside a cloud, offered death
for the first time.
The paths, their corners, had already been forged,
stones cut by the cold,
searching for the fountain,
the relieving breath
and Man — gasping — asked: Who are we?
to the stopped-up ear of the earth.

TIMES OF PRE-EXISTENCE

This voice, I know this voice.

An unfinished poem: people.

Now we have left the blood behind: We are just in memory,

a lost place of martyrs, the place

where statues have nails.

How the weeds have grown! Stupefied,

we see how the weeds grow

under this rich sun

and we wait. Masks!

This silence, I know this silence.

It's from the dead hand: when the sky

became red from exhaustion or shame,

because time grew late and not even the birds

replied.

This voice, this silence, this rich sun,

masks, everything

a point of contemplation more than anything — that doesn't

descend into forgetfulness with twilight: rather,

mystifying meteors and orgasms are welcome. How long

the sisters cry! And still you have not returned from the dead, Lazarus?

THREE

I am completely alone with God. Both
of us occupy and complete a space.
That's why I can't explain
the little noise from someone else
who is eating
in the room, so satiated
with God and me.

I examine the place inch by inch,
then the surface of the table
and there it is . . .
oh primitive nest! just in the wedge
maintaining the balance of the four legs.
There is where I find the termite,
the Third.

STOPLIGHTS

Look, one eye, two eyes, three eyes winking
one after the other, three eyes open,
shiny or dull, spots of green, yellow, red,
alert from a distance, or close, order you to go quickly,
stop, the danger of traffic jams, accidents, death, everything, stoplights.

Here, there, beyond, everywhere, the round masters,
severe and mocking, sharp (stinging), glowing, giants, gnomes,
but none are as big as them, talking constantly,
breaking, going, turning — doing what? — freezing, raining, sunny,
by night, with wind, weather's enemy, everything's enemy, stoplights.

Three buttonholes announce, bulging bumps, three lights,
three fires, three fingers, three lenses, three teeth, three hands,
three minds waylay what you are doing, where you come from, where you
    are going,
stop your feet, your heart, run out of gas, block the way,
okay you can go, now it says yes, now no, or maybe, stoplights.

And not knowing what to do, if it's this or that, or now nothing from nothing,
or ramming, colliding, wounding, killing, fleeing because
everything is as it is, the same sadness, the same heaviness, the same trivia,
the good, the bad, the seconds, and just like that, like them, the three colors

with cat eyes, dog eyes, with lamb skin, with the voice of an old man,
all I am is a rifle that doesn't fire, an uncertain front,
green hair, a yellow face underneath the red sky . . .
it all just becomes so crazy, the stoplights.

Kiss

Life is a burning, almost not touching life itself

and it changes us into coal, life that includes both

life and extermination! But without horror,

with interest in exquisite manure and the marvelous, slow fall.

I am the welcomed guest

and now is the time I pour myself deeply into the lips of this woman

who knows I will die.

How I Like It So

How I like it so — to write in a language
they say is dying.
What a feeling of peace and relief
taking it down to the shadowy spring pool
between her legs, the holy woman,
to the first brightness.

The sex opened and I opened my eyes
and I read on the bloody walls
this: I will speak!
And now I say, now that I know all there is to know
about love and thieves,
the deeper the death, the deeper it sinks into the earth!

KOAN

My name is Màrius and when I was born, legions
of demons helped me, among them my parents,
and among them recent ancestors, doubtless the good ones.
Still, I love them
and they love me, I know: goodness and death
advise and encourage me. All this I know
because I have to die.

Also the legions will call you by name
to be born, and the demons will help you,
and one of them will be me.

Ballad of God, River, and Sea

I saw God going down to the river *Besòs*,

the only time I ever saw Him and never again.

It was a clear morning, brutally clear

as it should be. Suddenly, the sky receded

into the pity, the color blue closed

the circle of thick rain and dark, thin head winds,

striving to take away the night's destruction.

But underground voices pray for the river to rise

and the frothy water foresees mud's evil.

The water had risen a foot

over His breath, dredging up stumps and cans, black hills

of a belly filling up with death, palm fronds, and rats,

everything all mixed together in the first question of the world.

I told myself that it must be Him, floating on oil and foam

from acids spilled by furtive narcissists,

lovers of spots and channels: God went to the sea and

I re-lived the old story

about the first who would be misled on top of the mountain

at the Asylum of the Holy Spirit from which

He would run away down the sad streets of Saint Adrià

where the hunger and the damp would make him sick,

afterwards, more pale and thin than the purity,

for sure, tubercular, spitting blood on both banks of the river, or He would wait for — blooming, grateful — the garbage and weeds,

but the storm comes. Therefore, it must be like that

and now all this washes out to sea. He did that for three good reasons:

to not make the same mistake of being seen again, to heal himself

with iodine and salt, and to remember the lost immensity.

There, at the mouth of the river, God will enter the circle of golden oranges,

and He will be pleased that the fish and the moon were one,

and He will meet old Ulysses, who never came home

and with whom He'll repeat the circumnavigation of our souls,

also made of water.

ONE DAY I WAS WRITING

One day I was writing about how to write poetry
which really consisted in asking each name
what other name it would be: your name
is longing-for-someone. You wouldn't want your name to be a premonition
or a worm, would you?

The rain
is your name, so would you be named a tear?
All that was a long time ago
and the names never answered.
It must be that they were thinking about it.

Now it's different. I wouldn't write that.
I know that nothing, not even permanent
envy from others, can resist its essential effort — that's just the way it is.
There's no answer. It's pure indecision, just hesitation. And
many years have passed,
and every name is the dying ember beside
its first invariable meaning.

I think, after so long,
that poetry makes the lips of the earth mute
with just an adequate word.

THE END OF THE WORLD WILL NEVER COME

The end of the world will never come

    if I remember your voice
    and my voice continues on
    and much later still, faithful memory,

conjuring the darkness and gravediggers, ripping the imperceptible questions
from the blind eyes of the silence:
Where are you, where are you, where are you? And no answer,

only a flower rising from the earth.

MOTHER, DO NOT SCOLD ME

Mother, do not scold me.
Yes, I know I'm old, but I didn't do it!

I didn't do it, as I used to say as a child
protected by light. Why not say it now, sheltered
by shadow?

"Broken toys on the floor,
all scattered in pieces, you're impossible!" It's a lie! It wasn't me! It was him!

And it was always him, Mother, the same one who unmade the bed,
the father, the hairy monster
who robs us of the beauty.

Maybe it's just and right: we owed him our breath,
smooth skin, even
the right to love us. But I didn't do it, Mother, you see that now, I come now
little by little, with a cane.

An Entire Sky

An entire sky
enormous and excessive,
just to put in a dining room.

An entire sky
profoundly wounded for a plate on the table.

For a pregnant belly,
for a contracting anus,
for a soul with false teeth and a forehead with wheels.

An entire sky and death.
And I can't tell it from an egg or a chestnut.

MOUNTAINS

There isn't anywhere in the world
a mountain
for the gods — or at least
no one has ever come back to tell us.
Just these little summits of orgasm,
the only consolation for their children.

[I TIE A KNOT IN YOUR CORD...]

I tie a knot in your cord and tie it to my womb
where you don't suffer the light. The day
is still very clear and waits outside
until you can see without being blinded.

I have swaddled with water, with swaddling clothes made of water,
dressed without stitches inside the basket,
new water that holds your body,
the future nakedness of water,
midday where continents are affirmed,
the summits melt, the coasts are sighted.

I tie a knot in your cord and tie it to my womb,
break its margins for you and bring you close.
Time is open and waits outside
until you can come along barefooted.

[SOMETIMES WE SIT ...]

Sometimes we sit

facing the same way.

Other times,

in the opposite direction,

we see the lightning

return

our way.

[LONG DISTANCE ...]

Long distance
takes on the swiftness
of the track
that comes
to join
and fly through the wind of landscapes
of the river Ebro
and concentrates on a point.

Now there is a story along the way
and it implies the degree
of movement
which is marked
and sustained.

It shakes the glass
and vibrates with the windows
where we trace the north.

[WE DO NOT TURN TOWARD THE LIGHTNING ...]

We do not turn toward the lightning out in the suburbs

for all those streets where midday

turns poverty still larger,

more deaf, the silence more neglected.

Truth isn't beautiful, nor does it have to be.

The human, stammering among words,

spells losses, losing all sense,

enlisting tried and tired words, repeating

all too humanly unsatisfied and sleepless.

The human talks to us of faith, breaks promises,

foretells goodness, and the voice returns to us.

[PAIN ASCENDS ...]

Pain ascends
to the muscles,
suspicion,
the actual promise
on the other side
of sense.

We have to wait
until the first lightning dwindles
from the light of the eyes.

To night
belong the things of night;
shadows of day
belong to the day.

[INSIDE ...]

Inside,

time is calculated,

perfect, rigid,

to assist the breathing,

regular, measured,

with the exactness of a metronome

like the time

only God was in charge

and took

from the softest, artificial breath

that most regular rise and fall of the thorax,

mechanical,

alien,

registered.

Antònia Vicens

His Feet Always Hurt

My father's feet always hurt.
He limped to every shoe store
looking for comfortable shoes
to help him carry the heaviest loads
of cuts, wounds, and scabs from the sea.
He never found them.
He had to go shoeless, with his wristwatch
and the knife in his pocket for slicing bread and tears
and a pale face like the foam
that so often rides the waves.

He always told me:
"I had no childhood."

He couldn't get that off his mind:
"I learned to write my name at the front.
Bullets shrieked shooting stars of blood
when I was learning to write my name.
I didn't want to be just any worker."

O

And my mother said:

"He's a smart man. It's a shame

he doesn't know how to write. You

have to go to school, Antònia. Daughter, you

don't have to be ignorant like your father."

And her pale blue eyes washed across her cheeks when they flooded,

   crying for his absence.

DESOLATION

Father didn't know houses or even people from that narrow street.

No one boasted with their chins in the air to tell him:

Joan, have a nice day. It was as if his expression had melted.

As if he had lost his name.

It was enough to see him sitting at the small table.

Engrossed. Alienated. To look at his swollen feet was to know he prayed

with all his soul:

Help me! Oh sacred whores!

It was enough, seeing his eyes that were not so green anymore,

to know he was emptying himself

like the emptying and slow death of a rock crab in a broken abode

when taken out of the water.

Sometimes, he looked up at the sky
like a beggar extends his hand to people passing by ...

just to read the stars, to ask
if god, who so often got trapped in the nets, was
simply a snail or a sea turtle.

SNAPSHOT

In the plaza, my breasts under the sweater
defy the photo.

I was very young when someone suddenly snapped my picture
as I descended the church steps. (In the background, the bell against the sky.)

Men were leaving the bar with schnapps in hand.
Smiling,
etherized and concupiscent.
It was on a Sunday.

Among all of them, the only look of innocence was the look on my father's face,
sea water and sails.

He didn't know what it was to be rich, but he knitted nets:
Catching time,
retrieving the exact minute of purity.

He always used to tell me:

"When I was thirteen, the sea already hurt my back.

When I was fifteen, I knew nothing of brandy, let alone aspirin."

And my mother said:

"He's still dreaming about the shores. You don't have to be

like your father. He was always

easily seduced."

And a strung-up bunch of moaning was stuck in his gums

like hooks on trawl-lines stuck

in coral.

[BECAUSE YOU HAVE REACHED THE WATERFALL OF YOUR LIFE ...]

Because you have reached the waterfall of your life
so that when someone asks you what you like, you answer
I am happy on the day of the week I change
the bedsheets and the bed smells
of childhood.

Only Seagulls

I couldn't see anything
except black seagulls
in the bloody scab of the dying sun.

The shape of my father was lost.
The shape of his boat was lost.
The rising starlight had crossed the horizon, smashing away time.
Then it rained over the sea.

Rain and wind formed eddies of water: footsteps
to catch the sailor's dreams. But they
could not catch his voice when he said,
"I have arrived at the country with the finest pearls."

THE WAYS

(Where there were the ways of childhood with globeflowers
and asparagus . . .

now proudly
there blooms tar.)

(Not even the stones grow.

They have filled up the life on the cradle side of the road with cement.)

(This has halted the transmigration of souls:
Now almond trees no longer bloom over the sidewalks of the ways.)

(Emptied, broken, castrated:
The anus sewn up tight.*

They wanted to change the way of women from sunrise to sunset in a vagina

in a flower

mute.)

Cotorreta cul cosit is an expression that refers to sexual restrictions placed on women, and this is impossible to translate.

SERVITUDE

You end up bending your back over the blank page.
If you don't write, the words burst
inside your mouth

                  flooding your breast

                              your guts. You

who open the windows
to let in desire. Or how you say kill
the thirst to find grace.

INEBRIATION

You grew up with the apostles among boats and
nets. You attended the wedding at Cana with them
and drank the miraculous wine, marinated in the candles' euphoria
that poisoned the ambience. (It had been a war. The wine
and the blood tasted the same.) Also, you
played with angels: those who fly around in the air
and those who are just shadows of the dead.

[UNTITLED]

Then the immensity returned   across the sea

a row of seagulls and the tail of a shooting star

in the sky, a flight of fishing boats and its wake

you concentrate on looking for supernatural visions

but immediately you let them go

if you rummage   corpses float to the surface

it's that sometimes a fisherman's

line breaks

and you remain at the bottom

of the sea

with the hook stuck

in your gums.

from ALL THE HORSES

When I was a young girl I wanted to be an Amazon

the guilty one   the Martini ad

the woman in a tulle dress

who crossed the sea's infinite line

mounted on a white

mare   it was said she has cancer

and will not survive the summer   then I wanted to be

a winged horse

galloping in the saddle of Death.

DISTANT WATER

I feel it from far, on the roof,

on the leaves intertwined

by twisted spear-like branches, down to wet soil

like the skin of a newborn, inside the temples

that burst with the weight of a deaf night.

I feel it from far, on the gnarled trunk

of the fig tree, on the stones that wear the faces of my dead.

I feel it under my feet, a fiery white,

pricking my fingers, and the gesture you can guess

under the parched skin.

I feel it as it strikes the pavement

where you walked and it guides

the soft steps before they melt.

I feel how it penetrates

the hidden roots where your bones are —

until they sprout.

I feel it cross the waterway at the farmhouse,

sticking its claws into the fertile garden walls,

climbing the mute willows

while fog rends the bramble in the orchard.

I feel it from far off. I know it embraces you

and falls, always slow,

over your eyes made of mud.

All the Seas

To be one field means to be all fields
with flowers and wheat or apple trees
and pomegranates by the road.
To be a sea means being all seas,
the essence of blue in serene inlets
and to navigate forever without a course.
To be a branch is to be all branches,
birch and ash, willow and cypress —
to draw new paths in unexplored skies.
One book is all books:
light of the cosmos, letters of thousands
of existing alphabets, lost or not yet come to be.
One voice is the voice of all those who do not speak,
the voice of the forgotten, the voiceless:
it is yours and mine.
One living being is all living beings:
The eyes of one are all eyes,
the hands, all hands.
We live in each voice, die in each body.

THE REVERSE WAY

There is always the possibility of leaving home.
—Joseph Brodsky

There is always the possibility
of coming back by the same steps —
quit being a mother and woman and child
and wrapping up myself like a snail
in a forgotten womb.

Also, there is the possibility
that summer could be over,
going and returning at a bad time,
and the heat inviting refuge
in a cave of pines.

There is always the possibility
that the roaring of the beach will drown
the noise underfoot
and winter return
and a little ice on the ponds — very little — ,
the wind jumping between legs
like lightning crossing the twilight,
going and returning at agreed times,
sheltering ourselves under the light

or in the night which is so long.

Also, there is the possibility
of walking under the poplars
on the shady path
where blackberries have rotted,
seeing an oriole's nest
at the tympani of the river
or the wing of a stray duck
clawing at the womb of the moon.

There is always the possibility
that the pain that's always there won't come back
without lapses or truce:
A dagger always inside.
Feeling that life snakes about
in the streets
and it tells me good-day on each corner
while I'm going the reverse way:
from the past to the womb, from the womb to nothing.

Francesc Parcerisas

NOW THAT THEY ARE SLEEPING

Now that they are sleeping
I would like to be the melted gold
or the apple cut in half-moons,
that the afternoon were slow for those who are sick,
and the quiet night, benign and without restlessness.
That the light were gentle always
now that they are sleeping
with a knife to the chest
— because they certainly feel it —
they could face the inevitable
and know the fear or terror of one's self.
So, now that they are sleeping,
they can see the body that sleeps
and the body that loves, cautiously —
and, beyond the body, touch the time
that will be its own: a cloud of nothingness
that time condemns us to. A fishing bird
in a city park is also a dream,
or a monster made of mud which is melting.
I am grateful for the roots that now sleep in them
to complete me. I close my eyes
and it is the sea and they who sleep
and the waves coming in and going out, separating us
past any good wishes.

Colors

Now that I am teaching you how to clean the brushes

in the soapy palm of your hand,

I see as the colors dissolve

an old order of things.

That which helps the imagination

now erases it, like years erase

the black skin of all words

which are only real inside us.

Strongly you rub the brushes with soap

until thick foam

dissolves the oil from the hand

and leaves the flesh soft, numb,

like a pink, innocent palette,

like the white smile of the dead,

like the cobalt blue that is the future,

or like the mahogany light of memory

where the infantile illusion watches

the walls where you hide your fears.

Story

I am fifty-five years old
and I see the chocolate night.
The sun sets slowly
behind the honey, almond twilight
and, from one side of the wall to the other,
the insatiable thoughts
give up trying to tie the tie
and double over from the odor of gangrene.
Children run down the street
chasing a yellow ball that screams
like a sugar candy moon.
I, who had never seen the ogre —
not in the alley of gray sewers,
nor under streetlamps of passion
made of marmalade —
know that this age gives me a quiet fear.
Now, suddenly, in an extended hand,
the thin bones of a chicken:
a piece of candy that time
licks in a cage between the bars.
Memory is ravenous
and reasoning is bread crumbs
that don't know how to tell me

how the world was

and they hardly remember who I used to be.

BALCONIES

Hanging from the balconies like a fruit,

a garland of bluish flowers which are socks.

The sun twists in the trunks of wisteria

and makes skeletons of circuses in the shirts.

A distant voice tells me: "There are a lot of insects

and birds," and I give myself a gift of words:

giddy up! giddy up! giddy up!

Behind a closed door, some hands play,

mixing mud and soil. The towels

collect the words from the sand at the beach,

the cries of joy that frighten ...

On the balcony there is a man in his undershirt,

leaning on the balustrade. And gaping. The dogs

chase each other on the street, the pencil traces

the map's contours: The blue is today,

the yellow is the future, death is purple.

I copy the past to save time.

I stretch out my hand,

I have smoke between my fingers

and the afternoon takes on the shape of old porcelain.

No one remembers the words as well

as the little breasts of a girl.

I'm going out to the balcony to watch those hours

that were not mine. And see all the penetrating words

that still aren't finished,

like strong wine in the order of the poem.

THE MEADOW

Having just finished planting, he had

little signs tied to the trunks of all the trees. And the signs say:

one tree for each grandchild, and each great-grandchild,

one meadow for when they come someday,

one botanical memory that will watch you grow.

So the children are nurtured by memories hidden

under the stones, or if the year has been good, then

they will reach a hand up to the sky or eagerly gather

the forbidden fruit that experience still hasn't had time

to rot. But maybe,

more simply, what the experience wants is to vanish . . .

the experience that makes you plant the trees

in the deep ashes and, the roots arisen,

settled in your mouth — sweet apple — now green and bitter —

and contemplate the high meadow and the slow flux

of tides that oscillate, beautifully, like the slow breath

of a dream

to make us understand

that the brownish mud of deception and guilt

is also forgiveness, happy and ancient . . .

the meadow has been planted for us forever.

THE OLD TREE, II

What there was in the tree is still there
because everything that was still is.
You only need the hand that rests there
and tells him: "Come."
Because the hand is him: tree and thought
and time that wants you and searches for you
to survive in you
because if you think, then you are,
and if you think about the emptiness
of being, you are empty.
Give me your hand to bring me certainty
almost as if the will and existence
were together, joined as lips
where we are, the two of us, one tree.
Where I am your bark
and you the emptiness that burns me.

THEN

Then with hands
caress his head,
then with arms,
embrace his body,
then with a finger
tear out his eyes,
then with teeth
chew his liver,
then with claws
shred his memories,
then with nipples
let him suck the milk
of hatred,
then with the tongue
she said Lord, Lord,
all I do, I do for love
because you have promised us
that this bread is your body
and this wine is your blood.

The Moment When Something Is Enough

In the moment of plenty
there are moments that are enough:
enough narrowness of very
and enough volcanoes of little,
enough appearances of morning,
enough night from out of its storage, and glasses,
enough passion from the street, detergents,
tunnels, feather dusters, Friday's wolves,
urinals at the bottom of the towers
of memory . . .
Enough of almost,
enough of not very enough of everything,
enough of little by little.
He has swollen feet and wrists
and he breathes in a plastic bag.
He has a bloated stomach,
a gangrenous stump,
emphysema that chokes.
Enough of worms, veal, shark,
of the green bird that warbles.
Enough of enough, enough of silence. Now
we divide the brightness
from the shadows and we say:

How different the first day was,

we should return again.

The world is poorly made, the toast burned,

enough of eyes and of crystal,

enough of families in a garden.

It is not necessary for anything to begin, enough, enough.

FOLDING CLOTHES

I don't know how to go about the words.
Is it a common well where the boys look for water?
Now I fold your clothes:
they're old and worn, and comfortable,
good for wearing around the house. And you are
in each fold.
I see your eyes, the holes,
and I see the seam of your back,
the sleeves the color of your hair,
a button that is unfastened with joy
and the hem where my fingers will be your hands —
reddened, worn like a golden coin.
In this way, do we understand so well
how time drags us to the
wells of truth? In what moment
does the rag become a nuisance?
Throw the bucket down the well and listen
to how it fills and grows heavy,
holding the hidden weight of water.
I fold again,
the drawer emptied of your things
as if the drawer never severed my fingers.

Joan Margarit

1960*

I leave on the Rambla
a pedestal in a bay window
covered with banana trees
and a tourist's postcard of winter among the branches.

The old Cafè de l'Òpera is faithful
to the shadows owing to a language
born already captivated
by the reading of *Les Fleurs du Mal*.

When I was studying architecture,
that lingered inside me:
Baudelaire, nights with whores and literature.

And also an angel who, cracking open some doors,
has returned to rekindle, faithful, with a will of its own,
clouded mirrors and dead flames.

---

*Note: Margarit's original is a faithful Petrarchan sonnet. This is a popular form in Catalan literature, far more popular than in English literature, where the Elizabethan and Spenserian sonnet forms dominate.

MOTHER RUSSIA

It was the winter of 1962:
In bed, I didn't turn off the light
until the first sign of clarity from dawn.
I was reading Tolstoy non-stop,
imagining those far forests — as a dog barked
from some yard — fabulous sleds at night.
It snowed in Barcelona that winter.
Silently, the snow surrounded us
with soft flakes like a glass case,
and when better weather came, you, Raquel,
were already beside me
with that clear face of Anna Karenina.

Joan Margarit

MELODY

You love slow jazz when you're alone
and it burns its black fire in you.
The sax begins the conversation:
slowly describing
a dead bird in the road
and how autumn rain
slides off its gray feathers,
tender for children who have all grown up,
for the family dog who disappeared one day,
tender for the aging parent
standing beside a field of mature wheat.
You love the slow jazz when you're alone.

Woman from Segarra

Sweet grapevines of songs my grandmother sang to me at dusk
when we came back from the garden
by the irrigation ditch.
On the wires of death there are sheets
hanging with the wash,
but only silence answers
if I remember the breeze through the cane,
the pureness of dry air
and songs that spoke of vineyards.

The kindness in her eyes, the patience
in her wet hands that she always dried with her apron
when opening the door.
I slowly open my eyes and see this land from the past:
Ruined vineyards on the hills covered with frost,
the fields of Sanaüja, the coldness of the first rays of that sun.
Those days of the winter of 1942 when the sun rose
like a black heron.

POEM FOR A FRIEZE

There was a drawing on paper so fine

that it rose in the wind.

From the highest window to the far distance,

streets, the sea, years (that can never be recovered),

I have looked for it on the beaches in winter

when lost drawings are more sad.

I looked for it in all the ways of the winds.

There was a drawing in pencil of a girl.

God, how I looked for it.

In the Middle of the Night

The air is freezing,

so cold the nightingale won't sing.

With my forehead pressed against the window,

I ask my two dead daughters

for forgiveness

because I rarely think about them anymore.

Time has left dry clay over the scars. And besides,

when one loves someone, forgetfulness follows.

Light has the same hardness

as drops that fall from frozen cypress trees.

I place a log, stir the ashes,

and the flames flare up from the coals.

As I'm starting the coffee, your mother,

from the bedroom, smiling, says

What a wonderful smell. You have risen so early this morning.

Self-Portrait

What is left of the war is the old cape

of a deserter left on the bed. At night I felt

the rough touch from the years that were not

the happiest in my life.

However, the past just being a brotherhood

of wolves, melancholy for a landscape falsified over time.

What remains is love — not philosophy

that pretends to be opera — and, above all,

not about a damn poet: I am frightened,

but I go on without idealism. Sometimes,

the tears slip behind sunglasses.

Life is just a deserter's cape.

BALLAD OF MONTJUÏC

I arrive before dawn to be there alone.
The gas tank lights are still on
and lights on the cranes in the port.
The sea faces the misty city.
Everything is the same. I think,
it's not worth coming.
But the truth is I come anyway, liking to walk
the ramparts to see the ravines and quarries,
the promontory with its gangrenous cemetery alongside.

It doesn't want to be a park with statues from another time.
It still guards its former lighthouses, executions, barracks.
All the signs are precise, paved on the memory of the walls
and etched on cypress trunks.
When passion excites me to feel
that I have lost some memory,
always the Montjuïc inside me startles me
to recognize my shadows:
vanquished loves like the remains of the guard tower,
and years from my life like bronze cannons
to melt the monuments of sinister generals.
Forgetfulness echoes like the deaf blows of the bodies
of brute animals when they fall into their mass graves.

I hide memories in a pit that guards,

under a bed of roses and tulips, the footsteps

of victims and their assassins.

Inside me, there are old trees

and green that surrounds the fountains

and kiosks, the folk dances.

Inside me, there is still festival music from the country,

the dark of clandestine hotels, eyes of the anarchists,

the city's hatred for military walls.

I arrive before dawn to be there alone.

The cascades without water look at me like

eyes running with mascara after a hangover.

Full of garbage, quarries

are strata deeper than luminous fountains,

the amusement park where the Ferris wheel turns

like melancholy: This is the past.

There are lost days. And I begin to love

— now that it's destroyed — that time

as it was, which then I didn't respect:

And I love this memory

that resonates in the wind between the steel cables

and the white sails unfurled over the stadium.

Monjuïc is the guilt in the middle of the city.

I rest my hand on the bronze cannon

while a silent mountain rises inside me

that buries the story of everyone.

I have arrived before dawn to be there alone:

Only a cold cannon, when I caress it,

is truly an indifferent wolf.

LIBERTY

Liberty is the motive for living,

we said, student dreamers.

It's the motive old people clarify now,

the only skeptical hope.

Liberty is a weird trip.

It began in the bullfighting rings

with chairs in the sand

for the first elections.

Liberty is dangerous at sunrise, in the subway.

It's in all the evening papers.

Liberty is making love in the park.

Liberty is when the sun rises

on a day of general strike.

Liberty is to die free. They are Greco-Persian wars.

The words *Republic* and *Civil.*

A king leaves by train into exile.

Liberty is a bookstore.

To go without your government ID

The prohibited songs.

A form of love — liberty.

Joan Margarit

SOCIAL LIFE

You have idealized the loneliness
of listening to music, reading,
going for a walk in winter to regard the sea.
But the loneliness is a rain
that stains the windows of this train of years.
Loneliness is that cruel word
for a bitter and frequent bad mood.
It's a law of the random, the dark, and injustice.
It's not having money. It's to be frightened.
It's sex, a strange false lead that
sports the cruelest mirror.
Loneliness is not having hope
for what you will live
or any excuse for what you have not.

READING POETRY

When I finish this book of poems
by Paul Celan, I know neither what he said
nor what he wanted to tell me. I don't even know
if he was pretending to tell me something.
Hermetic poets are terrified.
I place my hand on top of the closed book
and swear to reject this fear forever.
Because poetry that often starts out
as a landscape where we arrive by night
always ends up being a mirror
in which one reads one's own lips.
What good is a container if it's empty?
Silence and emptiness are for angels.
For fear of garbage
or for the garbage of fear.

A Christmas Letter to My Father

I was never a hunter. I liked to visit Biniguarda
with you to see the dogs run or the the partridges sing.
When we came back to Lô, we walked and listened to church bells.
The world was joyful and safe because you held my hand along the way.
At home with my mother, watching her cook, we found my brothers
and there was great joy and so many of us, and we all had dinner
and listened to the radio.
Saturday evening, I took a bath in a washtub, and later you held me
in the rocking chair.
With the humble faith of the poor, you told me, "Poncet, one day we will
be rich. We have land in Havana!" but to me that wasn't important
because I had you. At home you filled me with kindness with your blue eyes.
I was the baby of the family, the one who listened the most to your stories
about witches and dragons, or your fear-filled chatter about the civil war.
Many evenings you returned exhausted from the factory and spent
extra time on your feet cutting pieces of leather, up in your bedroom
till late. I read, voraciously, all of the old books about that famous uncle
from your side of the family, the one who was the confessor for two popes
and other ecclesiastics in Rome.
I see you always satisfied.
You were wearing an apron and you had a pencil in your ear.
I often went to see you at Ca's Toribios
and you kissed me, happy, and your mustache was scratchy.

When your salary was so meager it dissolved in the can,

you hugged mother and with a lively gesture you smiled at her,

"Maria, everything will be clarified!" and she clarified everything,

and we grew up happy.

You made us Menorquinos, and with facts for examples, you told us

that we have to be good people.

Don't be lost in the woods.

When you hear the bells as it gets dark

and you come back alone

on the paths of the dead, I will give you my hand

and I will come to your side

to hear your stories and hear you talk to me without fear

of the civil war.

I hope you are fine and there are newspapers in heaven

and you can hunt any time.

You didn't care so much about politics.

If you see God, tell him that He didn't clarify anything,

that between war and hunger, He left a frightening world.

Christmas is a sad time for me, and it's as if the nativity scenes were missing

the old joy. Their little stars are dim and the figurines of shepherds are

   not smiling.

Always there is a worm in me that gnaws and it hurts.

Since you've been gone, I've felt the weight of a terrible emptiness

and I don't want you to die, father, anymore.

ORIGIN OF THE WORLD

Courbet

Like animals in heat

in the universe of symbols,

vaguely one time the flame lasts

like a mirage

for the world, greedy for sex,

anxious for sex,

restless for sex,

poking into the body's wound, searching

like atavistic mutants

between whimpering and kissing

to feel alive.

BIBLE STORIES

Religio perperit scelerosa atque impia facta.
— Lucretius

I. Adam

You give me, thank you, Eve, this new kind

of apple, and I am sick of eating fruit.

Today when we were asleep I dreamed

the taste of a new pleasure, which is to say, sex.

What would you think if we dropped all this business of snakes and apples?

How about we lie down naked and enjoy each other?

It's always the same here. I think this stuff about the tree

of good and evil is just a way

to say there are limits, that we can't do anything

we want if we want to stay in paradise,

but free as we are with our feelings,

thrilled by your beauty, I propose, Eve, a game

full of love that sets fire to the boring routine.

If you trust me, let me enter you

(I have had delirious thoughts about a couple of positions)

and you'll see how we'll be more human and happy.

II. Cain in the Land of Nod

God is unjust and I don't love him,
and I will take advantage of this place,
impose my language,
and I will get rich by spreading
little houses in order to market the land.

III. Noah's Son to His Mother

My father is screwed. Jahweh
has commanded him to build an ark where
he can gather the animals in pairs and we can climb aboard
because the world will perish. A great flood comes.
You must convince him not to buy any more wood or bitumen
and stay home, and calm down, and do your job of making baskets or
   urns from clay.
He's confused. I think it's his age, his six hundred years.

IV. The Foreman at the Tower of Babel

What is all this nonsense that nobody understands
and the work is behind schedule?
To be the biggest and strongest, if we want an empire,
it has to have the command of only one leader and one language.

V. The Lovers

Him:

I have grown old and nostalgic, remembering

all the wasted days, Rachel, that I didn't make love to you.

Her:

I have grown old and thankfully I remember, with a passion,

every day, Jacob, that we made love together.

VI. Isaac to Abraham

Tie the feet and hands, like a sheep.

You would have beheaded me to satisfy

the absurd plan from a god you have never seen.

You loved him more than your own son,

and I lost my faith in you. You're not my father anymore.

VII. Lot to His Wife, Edith

When everything is over and you are salt,

at least you will serve as salt for cooking or for curing skins.

The angels told you not to turn around

and all this happened to you because you're a busybody.

VIII. Joseph and the Pharaoh

One day this thing I do will be important.
The people will know why they are suffering
and maybe someone will get a job doing this.
For now, they have given me an ebony divan
where he lies down and I let him talk.
He tells me his bewildering, muddled problems
and he tells me, sleepily, all his dreams.
He doesn't know he wants to kill his father
or that he has a head full of tangles and phallic symbols.

IX. An Israelite in the Desert of Sin

Happy in his sky of meadows and fountains of cascading water,
Jahweh neither sweats nor needs to eat to live.
We search for a wind where we can put down roots
and this sort of sweet manna might make good business.

X. Solomon's Old Servant

The king, by inheritance of a luxurious empire, full of pleasures,
who has lived prosperously in enjoyment and good fortune,
now that he is old and tired, says everything is vanity,
and that studying and writing wise council leaves one exhausted, and

he, who was the richest man ever, without ever working, has
a harem where he has fornicated with a lot of girls, servants, concubines …

XI. Job

I still don't understand you and after so many tests
to know if we love you, it's just too much.
I don't punish a dog for licking its wounds,
nor do I cover up the scabies to show my faith.
What would you think if we were to just let it go
and talk to the devil who tempts us, and you, God, to buzz off.

XII. Jonas

Why have you sent me to convert them, Jahweh?
You already know all.

They are hard-hearted.
Let them kill each other
and hate among themselves.

A culture
of bile and bitchy-ness —
they don't deserve to live

nor can they save a language

spoken by Canaanites.

XIII. The Swineherd of Gadara

You think you're better but you have screwed me.

Why do you pretend to drive demons out of people,

putting them in the bodies of poor animals?

They didn't do anything, and anyway, they don't belong to you.

Who will pay me for this herd of possessed pigs

that you have cast — by your own fault — into the sea to die floating?

XIV. Lazarus

It's all fucked up. You have pulled me

from the tomb and have given me

some more years to live

to enjoy this sun that now sets while I see

the beauty of the fields

and I realize that I don't have any more future than life.

It's all fucked up. You can do miracles

because you are a god,

but I am human

and now I know, that is, what I used to believe

was messed up.

After dying

everything is darkness and forgetfulness.

There isn't anything more than absence.

XV. The Farmer to Jesus, Who Damned the Fig Tree

I don't know where you come from, but you have killed

the fig tree, and it isn't fair. If the tree doesn't give you

any fruit, it's because it's not in season yet.

In the country, everything has its time

and now isn't the season to collect figs, you sorcerer.

XVI. Judas

What the fuck are you accusing me for? —

you bastards — if everything went they way you planned!

I betrayed him

in order to accomplish all that.

What's worse,

you perverted the world
with Catholicism.

XVII. Pontius Pilot

Don't piss me off or use my name
as a symbol of a man who is undecided
in the face of facts that are beyond my control — you are of the opinion
that I didn't do anything, that I washed my hands like a coward.
I was only the magistrate, not the procurator,
and the priests dropped him in my lap already condemned.
Everybody knows that it was necessary to let one of the three go free
and the mob was very clear: Barabbas!

XVIII. Jesus on the Cross

I don't understand, Abba, if you are truly my father,
why would you let me be killed in this way. To make man
know you, love you, and adore you,
it wasn't necessary to allow so much torture.
The Gospels would have been sufficient
and a few more miracles tossed in.
In the end, this cross will be the symbol
upon which everything else will be predicated.

They will confuse joy with sadness

and they will make the words into punishments.

I'm beginning to doubt who I am, and You.

In spite of dying just to be brought back

and being able to show the world the existence of an afterlife,

now I see the truth — I'd like to be a simple carpenter, make a family,

and leave your business in the hands of the apostles.

XIX. Barabbas

Roman invaders liberated me

and he, who was innocent, got crucified.

Now, they say that after three days dead and buried,

he was a god and was resurrected.

I, who have been a bastard goat — not a sheep —

have robbed and killed without remorse.

I carry that man's cross nailed to my heart,

and his kind eyes look at me wherever I go.

XX. St. Luke

To write is to invent, and this Jesus,

who seems to you a mythical imposter,

will be, unwillingly or not, part of the story.

He already has groups of disciples who have founded

thousands of churches to adore him.

You label me naïve and doubtful, but he was

a Jew who loved to talk, a carpenter,

and he didn't do anything special

except die on a cross.

I know that one day what I write will endure.

But I only explain what I've been told. I never knew him.

XXI. The Apocalypse

Without the god of love, the unique god,

tied to the wheel of consumerism

(nothing about the beast of the seven heads,

the Antichrist, the seals, and trumpets),

people will live very badly, defeated,

in ugly places, and the world will be merchandise for them.

XXII. Fallen Angels

One can murder perfectly.
— César Vallejo

Don't kill anyone.
Don't succumb
to hatred or grudges.
Write, and shut up.
Peacefully, forgive everyone.

Don't tear away the covers in anger.
The stench of rotten
"blanched sepulchers," i.e., hypocrites.

You know that they exist,
breathing your air
and they even have children.

They are envious
and bite like snakes.

Don't be like them or want
to be blind by revenge.
It isn't worth wasting a word.
Everyone is just a puff of shit.

Goodness will save

the kingdom of this world

and writing will open the doors to wisdom.

Burn away all the pain

inside the verse, and leave

the vile or the spit — relegate it

to oblivion

and let them do whatever

and screw 'em.

Jordi Valls Pozo

THE BATTLE OF EBRO

for Rubèn García Cebollero

Outside the hive the soldier bees leave no one alive.

On the other hand, only empty infertile males leave the green satiated.

Of course, this is a matter of opinion.

One group took over the honeycomb with fixed bayonets.

The drones are like flies, maybe less insistent

but more effective. See how the bombs fall.

One side is winning without realizing it's a game.

It's okay to shoot someone just for thinking?

Maybe now I could change trenches, find one

that's more real, one with better benefits.

They have never liked honey — it provokes an allergic

reaction, even though they try so hard to eat it.

So it spoils. According to myth, Aristo was an expert rapist,

always taking advantage, even hurting himself

by being such a bastard.

For most, the war has taken us to the limits

of having to put up with others, thinking that

under those conditions it was better not to change your trench.

In the end, you have to meet each other face to face.

The tragedy of Eurydice has been a farce; incredulousness affirms it.

The scorpions of faith ... the scorpions are everywhere.

Take careful aim before you shoot.

Remember, in combat, your ammo is treasure.

If they have already reached sign number 705 and keep on at the same pace,

this will all be over soon.

No doubt the birds migrate north — better they don't hang around.

Old memories change to myths — indestructible marble.

War is sacred.

An ancient mysterious ritual.

The sons and grandsons of the fallen

have come to remember the penitence of a lost event

and they take photos to put into the pages of their vacation albums.

Birds migrate north, but sooner or later they return

and become part of the stones as fossils.

Better to be young and dead, tragic, pure, than to suffer

the deformed contradiction of a long agony, tyrannical and miserable:

Stalin, Mao, Castro.

Scorpions, under these conditions, are such tender creatures.

Solemnity opens the heavy door of a baroque church — the hinges squeak.

A deep voice expels tantric Latin — now they pray together

and Orpheus appears in aromatic and colorful incense.

From his mouth a swarm of bees flies out.

Who has dared to crown him with thorns?

Jordi Valls Pozo

—

FIFTY

It's not like shivering, but it is freezing here — down
to the bone. Does the heart beat?

It's hard to remember. You carry on,
years defined in a scribbled drawing
that you crossed out over and over.
Now the child — cruel judge who preferred the rules
over the game — is gone forever.

Distance is a paper that yellowed over time
and a pencil with no point — only going through the motions.
The orphan is emphatic and you tremble inside.

Apocalypse

They have packed their suitcases and have
    left by the door, leaving the key in the lock —
they didn't need anymore. Having given up,
    they walk a long way on the side roads.
                    The precise hour
comes when the circle closes.
They rest alone, in factory houses, trying
    to hide from the curious, between bushes.
No one bothers them. They are older
    than the oldest and now they've turned bitter.
They've had enough of what they've learned
    and they don't offer anything new to their children, either.
                Afterwards, because they want to,
they abandon the car and continue walking
    the desert dunes; exhausted, they leave behind sweaty clothes.
They don't care if they're naked. And their suitcases,
closed tightly, make good campfires on freezing nights.
Huddled together, now nothing identifies them.
They are what they say they are.
Later they groan, won't speak, but come close.
She, who won't stand for any more, returns the rib
    and disappears.
He, tired, cannot see the archangel with the sword that cuts off his head.
He is forced into submission.

To the Reader

Look, it's worth wasting your time.

Don't think too much. Come close.

The other side of the page is silence,

which, when it arrives at your ear,

trespasses the rumor of deafness. Another world

where you dissolve comes from peace and goes back

vibrating toward that lyrical mirror

which burns the soul by its indefinable nature.

The word tightens the knot

of the new story. With you, everything is possible.

Go and proclaim the passion where

success holds no importance.

Involution

Evil opens the waters
and deposits amphibian eggs
under the pebbles.

Evil, which is under the marble,
freezes the eggs
and slips into the shadows of my son.

That tree, of your own self,
opens in leaves.

Silence is the root of water.
Silence breaks the shell and is born against the root
of someone else.

Jordi Valls Pozo

THE PROLOGUE TO THE MYSTERIOUS ISLAND

Life always wins: you are the distracted one
from the flower to the root that trips up the will to resist.
You try so hard to resist the inversion of fading light.

The egg with no yoke touches the emptiness
of a shipwreck with ectoplasmic tentacles.
You witness forgiveness through the other door.

The eye is as close as an inflamed clearing
of low and heavy mist on the horizon.
The slowness of a fountain of mercury.

Listen to the figuration of the skin.
The curve of love, the arrow
that neither reaches nor touches the form.

You have to get dirty because nothing waits
in the shadow you project. What nest of dust
is utopia? The incredulous return

that forces the deafness of the factory.
And this blade that extends beyond the dreary threshold
of the façade is still standing,

warning us of the end, a snail climbing

up the cables of the machines.

The heart of its rhythm, a coin in the palm

of that child who begs for change, the unpredictable

vertigo of destiny, the ways erased

from bastard memory.

The skin the snake sheds

each time at the foot of each tear.

What good fortune — the colors when you raise your face to look.

And still you decide on what side the metal coin will fall,

an ephemeral sound.

Don't let the blind spots burn.

Manuel Forcano

NEW WORLD

No ancient chronicle had ever spoken to me about you,
or of your name, either,
or of the body you have offered me
like a friendly country
without barriers along its border.
No oracle was announced to me,
but you have appeared from the New World,
from one tomorrow that yesterday I didn't wait for.

The earth yearns
for vigilant eyes.

Love is a harbor
that finally reaches the ship.

COUNTRY

In your country the sun burns everything
and you have come searching
for shade.

   In my country
the sun sets very early
and I have come, thirsty for light.

The hunger of that bread of thirst
has vanished
in finding each other.

THE ELEVATOR

Everything depends on where you start
— you said.
Love goes up and down
the stairs — from the basement to the roof — in the skyscrapers.

Sex, the elevator.

You Feel the Body

You feel the body
like a mountain that gives its stones
to make into houses. You feel the tenderness
of a statue in the hands of an archeologist.
The joy of a sundial
at dawn. The joy of a well
that finds the one who fills it with water.
The delight of fallow land that receives the plough.
The pleasure of a cloud that, at the end, knows
the sky it passes through. And you see
how the waves break against the shore
over the sea.

When we love.

I Don't Recall

I don't recall the bus number for the Nile

that brought me to your side.

I don't remember the name of the street

your house was on, nor am I

so sure of your name.

I don't remember how many floors I climbed

to your terrace

or if I knocked on the door

or if it was open. I don't recall

which month of summer it was

or how many days I stayed,

the river's wide horizon and you in my eyes.

                  Maybe

it was only one day.

But I remember every day.

SUNFLOWERS

Maybe touched by some grace,

time has granted us

long enough

to make something so short that

we were living opposite that evil fist —

those two happy beggars

who give each other charity.

                                  Since we left

like an abandoned gold mine:

the derailed wagons,

the dark tunnels,

and the songs of the miners,

mute.

It's true,

we launch without knowing the waves,

but when I think about it I smile

and I move blindly

like a sunflower

bending toward the sun.

HYDRA

Once
you had the name of one love on your lips
like the name of a boat
on a bow
with big letters,
like an island printed over the blue
on a map of the Aegean.

What an island so small
for a love so vast.
What a love so vast
for so few days.
What few days
for a memory so vast.
What a memory so vast
for a poem so small.

[BITTER SILENCE ...]

Bitter silence on the lips.
A rumor of mirrors in the rain.

Bitter silence on the lips.
A rumor of mirrors in the rain.

Soft fish, frightened:
the mere joy of bright glass on the skin.

Like smoke from a flame,
so too love vanishes ...

I find a desert
in the mirror.

A dark whisper. A gaze. Listen,
a cry on the horizon.

Far away it's raining cracks.
The dust of summer dies

in the frozen dust of statues.
Someday everything comes back.

Josep Piera

With what face of ivory
or bright emerald?

[FAR AND NEAR, LIKE THE NIGHT...]

Far and near, like the night,
a chalk wall, a pointless key.

Ancient rumors, no. I don't want
from the sea a mouthful

of muffled old sobs of beyond,
that eye or knife of silence

that day, that sea, that place
where rain cries out in the distance ...

So fragile, the foundations
of love are memories.

[THERE ARE TIMES WHEN EVERYTHING FALLS APART . . .]

There are times when everything falls apart.

Slow glass,
the dead fall into a lair of gray matter
like the body of silence,
a mirror of before when they were beautiful, now old.

There are times
when everything falls apart. From hands fall
marble souls like cold poems or stones
and eyes change into wells,
all silt and all fear.

Night falls like a lair.

[Now ploughs the gentle breeze ...]

Now ploughs the gentle breeze
night's hair
like a hand, the smooth sea,
a tenderness!

He said — you know — idly:
Where are you from? What party are you going to
with braids of stars that fall
like a river from a high mountain?

And the voice wants to see flight,
seed of those distant lips
for planting, still.

Now, now with the veil
of dew, a gentle breeze dresses
the pale body of dawn.

[Magnets . . .]

Magnets
They call me to their embrace.
See
Of course you see
Not the whispering mantle of pine forests
Nor the oleander
Nor the reeds
Nor the song of river stones.

Every voice should be loved.

They can never arrive at music
The words, snow
Always far from the touch
Or sound, like the sea of the harp.

[LIKE GREEN SPIRALS ...]

Like green spirals
of summer flagstone,
                    like the woods in the evening
sparrows are flames
and flames are memories.

Pieces of childhood: the long
road of terror. Rusty ghosts,
wheat fields
and terrifying stories about people with tuberculosis.
Yellow ships made of bark,
grief and silence. Nothing.
All paths end in a ravine.

THE SIMPLE LIFE

You don't have to go very far
or walk barefoot on paths full of broken glass
or drown in the sea to drink light.
The light, that mythical language, a metaphor of wisdom.
What you're looking for is in front of you.
You don't have to take a boat to enjoy hell.
You don't have to go so far —
whether it's a chasm, a shortcut, a cliff, fire,
you don't have to run away. Look, it's there already:
things, skies, worlds, words,
horizons, jails, beings, walls.
You don't have to go very far.
Only a glance or a touch erases the distance.
To love is to know.
The miracle is inside us.
You don't have to go far.

Nude with Landscape

See him, hidden among the dead leaves and brambles, naked

beneath pine trees, reclining,

facing a bit of sky that dazzles —

his only reason is to be a splendid body. See him.

You can see the land for miles, a joyous lamp.

> A quail flies up, wings extended,

> and hovers in front of your eyes.

The rest is mountains, fields, and vineyards,

thickets, green patches, everything soaked in sunlight

> where his hand rests at his side.

Some flies draw black circles around the young pink skin.

Is it summer?

Who, from an unseen flock, bears the light cowbells?

The ambiguity of art, an ancient marvel

on an immense wall of a museum and yesterday

I saw it as real, an image

from the past. Today, you're already pointless.

For all the memories you've carried from somewhere else,

which, no doubt, are not the ones you're showing now.

However, I'm full of so many words that are mine

that I would like to paint you again,

or, better, destroy you and start all over.

Josep Piera

A Fragment of Winter Cut from a Diary

A match lights the kindling and the shadows are
like burned paper. This way a small stone
freezes the marsh. The hearth. An obscure text.
Like that, all bunched together like grapes, seeds,
eyes reflect a fire filled with friendly eyes.
The blue smoke is full of voices and ships
from magic smoke.

Cut out the dream pouring out the darkest seal
like you see a rat made of light in the room —
it scurries away in terror and returns, pale
as porcelain that only the dust could love.
He isn't a drowned rat anymore —
seagull, seagull into night. Sea spray . . .
What rumor of ancient seas carried in the beak!
What dwelling so overflowing with mutilated memories!
What goes on gleaming with images.

A white corridor without any detail of furniture,
a precipitous silence, now marble and dust.
A dog curls up under the table.

A pile of firewood searches out the burning logs.

All night the eye of the bell tower has insomnia.
Fog covering the mast and crags forever green
on the horizon of someone's lips: lightning,
faces and dreams in perfect embrace.

Are we, too, inside the fire's portrait?
Are we? Little pieces ... little pieces ...
We ... fleeting sparks.

RE-READING THE DRAWER

My past, so fragile, like cheap toys from a fair,
and yet it's not mine, rather it's from
a sleeping infant who looks at me
with arrogant eyes, short trousers,
with the smile of a prince who brings peasants
to their knees,
from a faded yellow and joyful day
in an old photo.

Walls ...
Walls of powdered milk
forbidden, a high white crown of broken glass
and jasmine
empties itself out far away
like unobtainable snow.

We believe in a lie
that we are one and the same.
You with that insolent look of infancy.
I am only certain of my doubts.
You with the blue ribbon ...
I, with the night in my eyes, waiting for dawn.

A Moment

There are moments, brief and warm,

that a transparent clarity

like a glass in the air,

chaps and cracks the skin and cells

with the caress of music,

warm and bloody water.

Thoughts like glass

reflect a story or forget it.

You feel alive all the way to your fingernails,

and a shattered, harmonious movement of tempestuous waves

occludes an ocean of veins.

Cliffs of sensations invade my body.

You leave. Far from yourself.

Surrounded by fog,

such a strange ship

traversing open space and joyous places.

A moment. Music. You descend.

You see yourself bending over the signs,

the spectator of an anxious love affair:

the eager and naked gesture of writing:

the mysterious garden of words.

A fresh sound of memories
falling into the hands of a thirsty child
who wants badly to drink.
That delirious desire was left in your memory,
good friends at daybreak.

[Such melodious lightning crosses the waves ...]

Such melodious lightning crosses the waves,
deep canyons and cliffs ...
You write the truth of living beyond limits ...
the bright, fertile lands of the moment.

To fill the lungs of the present with smoke
To fill the balloons of the fiesta with wind
To carry the sobs in your back
To fill the wild throat with blue

Like a desert that grows palms
or tablecloths after a feast
the unusual page, always a poem,
an ancient gesture of battle,
a last summation.

Cèlia Sànchez-Mústich

ANOTHER WIN

I only know the extreme pleasure

to be a pawn that advances across the board

and arrives at the other side

and changes into a tower

from where I can see everything,

embrace everything, translate the language

of bells, of the mother vulture, of wooly clouds,

to take a breath

for only a moment, only one movement

before the other piece exiles me from the kingdom

that no longer needs anything.

Hotel Room

"Give love where there is no love
and you can find love" — said the saint,
not thinking of unhallowed hotel rooms.
Now, if I dare to go to any
hotel room, I'll never leave
because the web is too tight
or so implacable the honey, or
the injection of love so hoarded
that I would be stunned
between the door and the terrace,
at the foot of the bed, with one stocking
stuck at the knee,
doubting forever if I am
putting it on or pulling it off.

UNCERTAIN NAME

I didn't say "I believe in You"
because I believe
but in order to believe
— really — in an eyedropper
that makes drops
the moment you count them.
And I tell you, god,
that I don't believe that's your name.
It's only an alias.
You aren't a very powerful creator
of either heaven or earth,
just a bird flapping wings
in a hole, and maybe
the final erosion, the unthinkable flight,
and I say "god" and it is only the abbreviation
of the unknown word
and little by little, it's growing
inside a test tube
in a laboratory of ruins.

CHAIN

As a dog knows in advance his owner's epileptic attack

and barks to warn him to lie down and bite on a roll of cloth,

like this, my god, I alert you when you are on the verge of a fall.

I am your dog as I am a god to mine,

and who knows if you are the dog of another god

that maybe never falls unconscious and convulses.

Bark to the other god to save you, me, and my pup . . .

Bark to not lose a link of any chains

that bind up all beings, because today I breathe the same air

as the children who live in the sewers, and a vagabond pain

scratches my body, the grave of the owner.

Conflict in the Afterlife

How would it be
if the afterlife is carnal
— that is, sexual — will I meet you again?
What kind of leaf? What mirror
could split me or unfold me?

We could play the three huddled in a bed for two
or the two of us rolling around in a bed for three?
Other lovers also could slip into bed,
the ones who would write, who knows,
this same poem
of innumerable vortices
diffused between the sheets,
and would I be annoyed, silent, tender,
until I risk sharing you
with extreme rendition?

Or is it that we are always living this way
and didn't know?

Feliu Formosa

He Emerges from Water

to Miguel Anglès

He emerges from the water
with some oysters
that have been pried from the rocks.

She,
naked beside the inlet.

With a pocket knife,
he opens the shells
and both suck the meat
from each oyster.

Slowly, under the sun
after licking one another,
the salty, torrid skin
still holds some drops
of water after their baths
in a perfect sea.

I take a deep breath:
There is no conclusion.

Feliu Formosa

FROM THE WINDOW

From the window
I see how suddenly the incessant drops
of rain impose themselves
over the red tiles
of the terrace immersed
in a gray silence.

And suddenly
the tortured memory of everything I believe to be still pending
stops and wants to be ordered inside me
with this old familiar feeling
of duty which
I was not looking for.

Everything is left in suspense,
the light sound of the rain
falling on the red tiles of the terrace immersed
in gray silence.

VENETIAN ETCHING

The calm that comes from a corner

will never be mine

where the water splashes

in the narrow channels.

There's a boat run aground

on a narrow strip of land

next to a bridge

visible in the distance.

I see silence growing

and I welcome it in silence.

I feel urgently the need

for a body close to me.

Over the decrepit houses,

the graceful facade of a church

talks to me

about what lasts

in the life hereafter.

THEY AND I

And now I see myself as strange and do not recognize myself.
— Gertrude Kolmar

From the most remote place,

I am constantly encouraged

by the poems beside me.

Languages coexisted

despite the threats

of an unfortunate era

that created strangeness.

In echoes of the Orient

where minorities lived in fear,

there is ancient wisdom

delivered from extermination.

The profound look

of a Jewish woman keeps me company.

MANNHEIM, 1960

You, surrounded by green.

I, blind.

You with your dark voice

and I, speechless.

Only our hands touch

and we are far from the games and agendas

of East and West, far from home.

It's here

we have established an ambiguous understanding.

It only takes a few words

to destroy a poem.

A poem finds time beyond.

Desire is close to a red house.

Tomorrow looks far away to us.

What will become of us without bridges?

SECTION XV, *from* DEL LLIBRE *Semblança*

Change the perhaps
for the purely random
— Pedro Salinas

I recover my voice in the midst of bodies

that have randomly come between us,

between signs that will spur us to act;

a profound caress that engraves itself on us

forever because time goes on forever

recovering, winning against the fear

of losing it, and the fear is left behind.

We know because we can still be surprised

by betrayal: that fear of loss.

It's for this the randomness completes us

and like this it sums up everything: poems, kisses,

with the relentless constancy it has

which love and randomness want to add

and can substract neither forgetfulness nor boredom.

And the wheel of loves that make up love

begins to turn around us

and begins to impose itself beyond time,

against fear, the smile of randomness.

THE POEM NAILS

The poem nails
fibulas to pulp.

Divides
the fog.

Opens a little
the fringes of the curtain.

Sees everything fall
without form.

Stays with all
that has been inflamed.

Says who knows
about silence.

A TINY GOD

Give me the strength to abandon you utterly.
— Ausiàs March

You think that you are strong,

that without you there would be no children and no parties,

there would be nothing without the man who lights the fire in the garden.

You know that your anniversary doesn't start without you,

that we are civilized, that children don't have to suffer

for what their parents do.

I bring wine to the table, and conger and sardines

so you can go on roasting

a heap of quartered animals.

In the end, who will gather the eyes

that gazed at the skirts? Who will keep Leonard Cohen

company after the last person has gone,

the lights without ears with unfulfilled desires,

the dishes dirty with mouth stains, and you, drunk, satisfied,

throwing up while I gather once more

the crumbs in the garden and at the altar where the offerings have

   been burned

for the tiny god who lies between cardboard boxes?

Pay Close Attention

Costly, if the man is mismatched,
the voice of death is a melody to him.
— Ausiàs March

I have loved so much,

and I have earned so much money to buy things

that to live, I just go on

and avoid eating salt

and doing whatever I like.

Now I often think that I have become crude and ugly and so passive

so as not to feel friendly to friends, any friend, or hate myself too much.

But when you want to die, everything dries up.

You feel endless pain you don't invent.

It's there when you go for a walk, smoke more,

and you drink up the mini-bar and look at people

as if they were grazing like cows.

Careful, boy, pay close attention:

It's when you want to die that you could kill yourself.

Jordi Virallonga

AN ARCHITECT'S MIMESIS

Whoever built this house

never thought that I was going to hate you,

and the kids would only have one room

to drown out their screaming parents

with stories and hushed songs:

I ask you, please, keep loving me

as if we didn't exist.

We don't want to be a bother.

Whoever assembled this house did so with a foundation

of prosperous new years and family business

and didn't plan any shelter for the boxer

who heard a bridge falling behind him

day after day,

knowing that the winner

takes all when the bell sounds.

It's curious to travel without time passing,

to be twenty years older with the way

growing more narrow

on this road appearing under the headlights

with sudden stones, places

whose time is the absence of destiny.

Jordi Virallonga

———

For us, there is only a bad deal

on the sale of a house.

Architects don't know anything about love.

Like you, they draw plans

that whatever remains will never be there.

UNTIMELY

The strong north wind will blow
and all together, the skies will fall apart.
—Joan Roís de Corella

I can caress iguanas and mussels
and other lower animals,
plunge myself in coral seas,
but cannot sleep with you
this afternoon of the sea and north wind,
smoking beside the sunny window.

I say that all will end, and all begin:
The sea above, columns of the promenade,
storms and skies gnawing at my face.

You sleep without dreaming like fish sleep in water,
and without lying on the better side of my bed.
And I urge myself to surrender to sleep
the strength I yearn for when you have
reached the end.

I Have Washed My Hair

Never take for a friend a man who loves you.
— Ausiàs March

Today I washed my hair.
The day before I did the same thing,
but then I didn't realize
that death wasn't just a joke.

I deeply live the life I do not have
among the men I know, and afterwards I see indifferently
when I get to school.
I tell you I wasn't wrong
that this insipid place wasn't made for beauty.
Don't dwell so much on the past
or the warped windows of that motel
just to make it so late that I'll have to invite you to stay.

Our bodies are so used to each other
that it's too easy
to be together, or make love, or clean the house,
or like this afternoon, take the kid to the horse and frog park.
Today I washed my long hair
while you read the newspaper, and I thought
how ants live.

David Castillo

August

Nothing was like a stone house,
nor were the depth of those eyes
waiting for better times, some wind, some air.
You wished to regard the wind stirring the sand,
the river's current and the reeds that bend
until they believe they are sand,
sand so far from the sea.
You want to think about trains
spinning in illusions of children's faces.
You want to believe you are the screech owl and sing the echo
which never returns from the girls' dreams
across bewitched beds with ogres with fangs as sharp as knives
that comb the promises thrust inside of you.

There are days when the light of long afternoons
grows short, and light penetrates the smiling faces,
a shining brilliance, a summer storm
on the Delta roads.

They don't even know the luck
they stand to lose:
to master the moment
and surrender to it,

knowing that the future isn't worth a thing,
and neither are they the chords of a guitar
strummed at dusk, when there is still a little light
or the flight of a bird
making arcs under the blue
when you look up.

Think about the next day without more temples
than just those with jasmine flowers
or their perfume or the long street like desire
shaped like marble.

David Castillo

THE DEATH OF JOHN KEATS

I.

You tell me your head and heart are divided
as if they had ever been joined.
You make false, rational promises
to escape the circus
where you live silent in a world made of screams,
dwellings of the eternal dream of marriage
and proud, civilized Catalan boys,
democratic, well educated, successful,
with lustrous suits and that professional pose.

II.

I feel your boring future like a clairvoyant,
feel it perpetuate itself at the family dinner table
on death-like Sunday afternoons
and I see transient vagrants crossing streets
where you yourself wither away in a slow fire
in the hospitality for whomever, for convenience
and skepticism, like the terms of a mortgage,
friends for going out with, drunken lovers and doses,
mediocre doses of furtive romanticism.

III.

I know that God, so often outraged
and who made you in His image,
regretted leaving duplicates on the earth
but for narcissim did not dare to eliminate them.
Now, Pygmalion feels betrayed.
He prays for obedience
to who knows who or what knows what,
and stakes claims on love contracts,
vague and imprecise contractual bonds,
insured third parties,
a pact of affection against failed poems,
epic verses that become a reproach in the mirror.

IV.

Love which is not valued
over social order
is the song's corpse
torn from Keats whom you would repeat
with your faked bad memory:

"Dying is plenitude, richess.
My adoration would die
rich in the simple adoration of a day"

or a year, or an epoch, or a mirage

in front of your sad reality,

without any joy or self-esteem.

DOUBLE ZERO*

Like a cat with an open stomach
crawling in a way so as not to spill its guts,
my pride falls from the sky to the sewer
when I smell treason for love.
I don't care.

The great architect of the universe is a wretch
who knocks on the doors of paradise and begs for one more drink.
He can't persuade the doorman, Saint Peter, that old converted pimp,
when he whispers with parsimonious gestures that he's not been a good boy,
or even a good Catalan.
And Peter says, "You didn't believe what the wise men,
those politically correct Catholics, told you. Now you beg for booze?
I have nothing for you, much less
the price of admission with a free drink.
You should sell your soul to the one who doesn't want to buy it.
Also, I don't think you'll find him to be a buyer:
He is too busy selling happiness, little doses of happiness
for torn cats, reckless for love
or for an excess of vanity." I don't care.

The cat looks at his open wound,
a bleeding hole from a switchblade
like a shining moon in the silver spoon
where cotton swims in indulgence.

He accepts that the biggest danger

was always his own impatience,

but he will never tire of repeating the same mistakes.

With his seven lives rushing to the end,

dejected, he can't manage to balance.

When he sees the seven lives through half-open eyes,

he detests the affection the icons trickle,

those icons nailed up in the temple of Lezama, in the eyes of idolaters:

"Image is, for the invisible world, reality."

Also, he foresaw the intuited caprices

that gave Reason to the Rationalists:

tongue twisters that finally kiss your cheek,

amnesia or confession in a fixed phrase,

sun against sunglasses and the troupe of friends

who repeat themselves like friendship among drunks.

"The only thing that doesn't fail today is bad luck,

bad luck in the interpretation of the immediate past

when you conjugate your verbs, in letters I never sent you

because by that time I had stopped writing letters — old cats never send letters —

neither did I offer you any solutions to your female problems,

nor promises to calm you down,

or even a little sympathy."

What do you expect from a filthy, wounded stray cat?

———

*"Double Zero" refers to fine nylon stockings that are used in the production of high-grade hashish.

Meanderings

Summer doesn't descend over our love
although a cricket sings in the window
and you do not bathe in the calm sea anymore.
I go, feeling like ruin and decline
in the middle of the wrinkled scream, too often repeated.
Crepitating flags on the avenue,
some torn, others dirty,
like our decadence,
like the curtains in our dark apartment at *Fabra i Puig*
where I crawled to you
when you were dancing naked on top of the fridge
that we made into a closet to store everything we said to each other:
stupid unfinished symphonies,
from boring Rock & Roll groups
we listened to from a radio station with no interruptions,
loves and police nightsticks,
an unexpected pregnancy with a drastic solution,
a trip that finished in the town of Ronda
when our destination was the mountains of Atlas
and an excellent collection of mediocre friends
in a directory lost in a drawer.

Just as you arrived you disappeared
returning haphazardly to your life.

David Castillo

Every mile away from me made you remember me
more fondly, little bits of lazy memory.
You perceived me lightly, lost in thought, biting your lip
and then you would have quickly returned.
Was that your luck?

DETERMINISM

I run even though I'm not in a hurry,

I walk without strength,

I work without necessity, all day.

I love without a face

and I go to appointments with no assigned hour,

trying to find something I wasn't looking for

when I could have found it, but I didn't want to.

Now I drink without thirst.

I drink too much beer in the *Plaza del Sol*,

contemplating the toe of my shoe

as if it were a filthy sunset.

I see the waitress's neckline

and remember your voice without wrinkles,

your longing without reproach

and the warmth of your love

with no confidence and no compromise,

without a deadline,

the warmth of your old love like a reason for being.

ERRATIC FLAME

Feet over the planks of a bridge,

noise against the abyss that slips, metallic,

in perceptions like equivocations, abiosis,

fatuous anger that asks me about nothingness,

wanting violence that I forget to not repeat

what isn't worth it when the mountain avoids thunder

and the wind stirs like a beast the anti-aircraft antennae,

sails in the hurricane that changes into will-o'-the-wisp,

erratic flames, you,

when you explain in too many words, and

realizing that, shut up.

Before the Beautiful Sea

You dreamed an enormous cake made of clouds
when you were a little girl. And what is left over?
You aspired to live without problems.
And what happened?
You insist on not growing up
and you're not interested in the pain I give you.
And what do you have?
You can't make plans, can't decide,
you don't want to decide and you only live with fear.

Storms rage,
generations change,
and you grow old:
you don't want to heal the wounds
even before you've been wounded.

Poets' Bibliographies

Màrius Sampere was born in Barcelona in 1928 and died on May 26, 2018. His poetic works include *El hombre y el límite* (Proa, 1968); *Poemas de baja frecuencia* (Ediciones 62, 1976); *Samsara* (Prometeo, 1982); *Libro de las inauguraciones* (Columna, 1984); *Oniris y el tiro del cazador* (Columna, 1987); *El pájaro que piula* (Columna, 1990); *La taula i les estrelles* (Columna, 1992); *La canción de la metamorfosis* (Columna, 1995); *Demiurgo* (Columna, 1996); *Thanatos suite* (Seuba, 1997); *Si no fuera un secreto* (Proa, 1999); *Subllum* (Proa, 2000); *Las inminencias / Les imminències* (Proa, 2002); *Jerarquías* (Proa, 2003); *Mutaciones* (Miquel Plana, 2003); *Iconograma* (La Garúa Libros, 2004); *Diálogos con la ciudad* (Centre Excursionista Puig Castellar, 2004); *Nos encontraremos fuera* (Proa, 2006); *Otras presencias* (Editorial Meteora, 2008); *La ciudad sumergida: Obra poética inédita: 1970–2008* (Ediciones del Salobre, 2009); *Infinito* (Ubicuo Studio, 2013); *Nadie más y la sombra / Ningú més i l'ombra* (Proa, 2014); and *123* (Ediciones del Buc, 2015).

Teresa Pascual was born in Gandía, Valencia, in 1954. Her works include *Flexo* (Gregal Llibres, 1988); *Les hores* (Poesia 3/4, 1988); *Arena* (Ediciones Alfons el Magnànim, 1992); *Curriculum vitae* (Jardins de Samarcanda, 1996); *El temps en ordre* (Proa, 2002); *Rebel·lió de la sal* (Pagès Editors, 2008); and *València Nord* (Ediciones del Buc, 2014).

Antònia Vicens was born in Santañy, Islas Baleares, in 1941. Her works include *Banc de fusta* (Moll, 1967); *Material de fulletó* (Moll, 1971); *Primera comunió* (Moll, 1980); *La festa de tots els morts* (Nova Terra, 1982); *Gelat de maduixa* (Fernando Torres, 1984); *Quilòmetres de tul per a un petit cadaver* (Laie, 1987); *Terra seca* (Planeta, 1987); *La santa* (Laia, 1988); *L'àngel de la lluna* (Baula, 1997); *Febre alta* (Edicions 62, 1998); *Massa tímid per lligar* (Baula, 1998); *Lluny del tren* (Destino, 2002); *39º a l'ombra* (Selecta, 2005); *Tots els contes* (El Salobre, 2005); *Ungles perfectes* (Proa, 2007); *Lovely* (Moll, 2009); *Ànima de gos* (Moll, 2010); *Sota el paraigua el crit* (Lleonard Muntaner Editor, 2013); *Fred als ulls* (Jardins de Samarcanda, 2015); and *Tots els cavalls* (LaBreu, 2017).

ROSA FONT was born in Gerona in 1957. Her works include *Tres notes i el silenci* (Edicions 62, 1989); *Quadern d'Erinna de Telos* (Columna, 1989); *Com ombres vives* (Columna, 1996); *Aigua llunyana* (Viena Ediciones, 2001); *La llum primera* (Editorial Tres i Quatre, 2005); *Des de l'arrel* (Proa, 2009); *Un lloc a l'ombra* (Proa, 2011); and *Em dic la veu* (Llibres del Segle, 2016).

FRANCESC PARCERISAS was born in Begas in 1944. His works include *Vint poemes civil* (Ariel, 1967); *Homes que es banyen* (Proa, 1970); *Discurs sobre les matèries terrestres* (Edicions 62, 1972); *Latituds dels cavalls* (Lumen, 1974); *Dues suites* (Edicions 62, 1976); *L'edat d'or* (Quaderns Crema, 1983); *Obra poètica 1965–1983* (Columna, 1991); *Focs d'octubre* (Quaderns Crema, 1992); *Natura morta amb nens* (Quaderns Crema, 2000); and *Dos dies més de sud* (Quaderns Crema, 2006).

JOAN MARGARIT was born in Sanaüja, Segarra, in 1938. His works include *Cantos para la coral de un hombre solo* (Editorial Vicens Vives, 1963); *Crónica* (Barral, 1975); *Predicación para un bárbaro* (Prometeo, 1979); *L'ombra de l'altre mar* (Edicions 62, 1981); *Vell malentès* (Eliseu Climent/3i4, 1981); *El passat i la joia* (Eumo, 1982); *Cants d'Hekatònim de Tifundis* (La Gaia Ciència, 1982); *Raquel: la fosca melangia de Robinson Crusoe* (Edicions 62, 1983); *L'ordre del temps* (Edicions 62, 1985); *Mar d'hivern* (Proa, 1986); *Cantata de Sant Just* (Institut d'Estudis Juan Gil-Albert, 1987); *La dona del navegant* (La Magrana, 1987); *Llum de pluja* (Península, 1987); *Poema per a un fris* (Escola d'Arquitectes de Barcelona, 1987); *Edat roja* (Columna, 1990); *Els motius del llop* (Columna, 1993); *Aiguaforts* (Columna, 1995); *Remolcadors entre la boira* (L'Aixernador, 1995); *Estació de França* (Hiperión, 1999); *Edición bilingüe catalán-castellano: Poesía amorosa completa 1980–2000* (Proa, 2001); *Joana* (Proa, 2002); *El primer frío: Poesía 1975–1995* (Visor, 2004); *Cálculo de estructuras* (Visor, 2005); *Arquitecturas de la memoria* (Ediciones Cátedra, 2006); *Casa de misericordia* (Visor, 2007); *Barcelona amor final* (Proa, 2007); *Misteriosamente feliz* (Visor, 2009); *Intemperie* (Ediciones Rilke, 2010); *No estaba lejos, no era difícil* (Visor, 2011); and *Se pierde la señal* (Visor, 2013).

PONÇ PONS was born in Valencia in 1956 and moved as an infant to Menorca. His works include *Al Marge* (Moll, 1983); *Lira de Bova* (Colección Tià de Sa Real, 1987);

Desert encès (Quaderns Crema, 1989); *On s'acaba el sender* (Edicions 62, 1995); *Estigma* (Edicions 62, 1995); *El salobre* (Proa, 1997); *Abissínia* (Columna, 1999); *Pessoanes* (Bromera, 2003); *Nur* (Quaderns Crema, 2006); and *Camp de Bard* (Proa, 2015).

JORDI VALLS POZO was born in Barcelona in 1970. His works include *D'on neixen les penombres?* (Columna, 1995); *Natura morta* (Columna, 1998); *Oratori* (Tres i Quatre, 2000); *La mà de batre* (Caixabank, 2005); *Felix orbe* (Denes, 2010); *La mel d'Aristeu* (Aguaclara, 2013); *Mal* (Valparaíso, 2015); *Última oda a Barcelona* (La Garúa Libros, 2015); *L'illa misteriosa* (Meterora, 2015); *Violència gratuïta* (Edicions 62, 2016); and *Guillem Tell* (AdiA, 2016).

MANUEL FORCANO was born in Barcelona in 1968. His works include *D'un record a l'altre* (Premi Amadeu Oller, 1992); *Les mans descalces* (Columna, 2004); *De nit* (Moll, 1999); *Com un persa* (Tandem, 2001); *Corint* (Proa, 2000); *El tren de Bagdad* (Proa, 2003); *Llei d'estrangeria* (Proa, 2008); *Estàtues sense cap* (Proa, 2013); and *Ciència exacta* (Proa, 2014).

JOSEP PIERA was born in Gandia, València, in 1947. His works include *Renou: la pluja ascla els estels* (Tres i Quatre, 1976); *Presoners d'un parèntesi* (Libres del Mall, 1978); *Crits baden la tarda melodiosa* (Septimomiau, 1979); *El somriure de l'herba* (Proa, 1980); *Esborranys de la música* (Tafal, 1980); *Mel- o-drama* (Edicions 62, 1981); *Brutícia* (Libres del Mall, 1981); *Poemes de l'orient d'Al-Àndalus* (Edicions 62, 1983); *Maremar* (Edicions 62, 1985); *Antologia* (Gregal, 1987); *Dictats d'amor: Poesía 1971–1991* (Edicions 62, 1991); *En blau* (Ajuntament de Màlaga, 1993); *En el nom del mar* (Empúries, 1993); and *Cants i encants* (Ensiola, 2004).

CÈLIA SÀNCHEZ-MÚSTICH was born in Barcelona in 1954. Her works include *La cendra i el miracle* (Columna, 1989); *El lleu respir* (Columna, 1991); *Temperatura humana* (Columna, 1994); *Taques* (Edicions 62, 1997); *Llum de claraboia* (Pagès 87, 2004); *A la taula del mig* (Moll, 2009); *On no sabem València* (Tresiquatre, 2010); and *A l'hotel, a deshora* (Curbet, 2014).

FELIU FORMOSA was born in Sabadell in 1934. His works include *A la paret, escrit amb guix: Antologia de la poesía alemanya de combat* (Edicions 62, 1967); *Llibre de las meditaciones*

(Edicions 62, 1973); *Albres breus a les mans* (Proa,1973); *Raval* (Edicions 62, 1975); *Cançover* (Vosgos, 1976); *Llibre dels viatges* (Proa, 1978); *El present vulnerable* (Laia, 1979); *Si tot és dintre: Poesía 1973–1980* (Grijalbo, 1980); *Semblança* (El Mall, 1986); *Per Puck* (Columna, 1992); *Al llarg de tota una impaciència* (Edicions, 1994); *Cap claredat no dorm* (Pagès, 2001); *Centre de brevetat* (Meteora, 2006); *Darrere el vidre: Poesía 1972–2002* (Edicions 62, 2004); *A contratemps* (Perifèric, 2005); *El somriure de l'atza: Diaris II* (Perifèric, 2005); and *Papallona de l'ombra* (Pagès, 2018).

JORDI VIRALLONGA was born in Barcelona in 1955. His works include *A la voz que me acompaña* (Gráficas, 1980); *Saberte* (Laertes, 1981); *Perímetro de un día* (Laertes, 1986); *El perfil de los pacíficos* (Libertarias/Prodhufi, 1992); *Dos poemas en Turín* (Librería Anticuaria El Guadalhorce, 1992); *La vida es mentira no obstante va en serio* (Cuadernos Hispanoamericanos, n. 547, 1996); *Con orden y concierto* (Sa Nostra y Universitat de les Illes Balears, 1996); *Crónicas de usura* (Kutxa, 1997); *Llevarte el día a casa* (Ayuntamiento de Málaga, 1999); *De varia misérrima* (Arrayán, 2000); *Poesía en el campus* (Universidad de Zaragoza, 2001); *Los poemas de Turín* (Lumen, 2001); *Sol de sal* (DVD, 2002); *Todo parece indicar* (Hiperión, 2003); *Poemas de amor descortés* (El Toro de Barro, 2005); *Por si no puedes* (La Cabra, 2010); *Hace triste* (DVD, 2010); *La amplitud de la miseria: antología de poemas 1986–2010* (Caza de libros, 2013); *La transparencia oculta lo que muestra* (Arfo, 2014); *Incluso la muerte tarda* (Visor, 2015); *Amor de fet* (Pagès, 2016); and *Animalons* (Pagès, 2016).

DAVID CASTILLO was born in Barcelona in 1961. His works include *La muntanya russa* (Pagès, 1993); *Tenebra* (Proa, 1994); *Poble Nou flash back*, with Albert Chust (Proa, 1997); *Game Over* (Proa, 1998); *El pont de Mühlberg* (Proa, 2000); *Seguint l'huracà* (Taragona, 2000); *Bandera negra* (Sial, 2001); *Antología personal* (Sial, 2001); *En tierra de nadie: poesía 1980–2000* (Malaga, 2001); *Menta i altres poemes* (l'Esguard, 2005); *Downtown* (Icaria, 2005); *Esquena nua* (Proa, 2006); *El llibre dels mals catalans* (Columna, 2010); and *Doble zero* (Proa, 2011).

ACKNOWLEDGMENTS

We wish to thank a number of people who helped us along the way: First and foremost, thank you to all of the poets in this anthology, in addition to those writers and scholars already mentioned in our introduction. You were very wise in your guidance. Thank you to the wonderful staff at Tupelo, especially Jeffrey Levine, Jim Schley, Marie Gautier, and Kirsten Miles. Thanks also to Lucy Gardner Carson for your keen eye in the final hours. Thank you, Hunter McMinn, for catching a history error. Thanks also to Brent Terry for putting us in touch with our allies in the UK. Thanks, Janyce Stefan-Cole, for letting us crash with you in New York, when visiting the Ramon Llull office there. And thank you to all of you at the Ramon Llull Foundation for your incredible grant, and also your wonderful staff, especially Maria Cristina Hall and Maria Jesús Alonso Vicario. Thank you, Joaquin Costa, for giving us a free place to stay for several months in Barcelona. Thank you, Joaquin Nadal, for your artistic attention to this anthology. Lastly, thank you to Albert Ibañez Domenech at the Institute for Catalan Letters for putting us in touch with so many amazing people.

Translators' Biographies

Francisca Esteve Barranca was born in Castellón de Rugat, València, in 1947; then her parents moved the family to Barcelona when she was a few months old. She trained at *Escuela de Artes Aplicadas Massana* in Barcelona and became a painter. In 1984, she immigrated to Mexico City. She met Marlon L. Fick in 2009 and they married in 2011, thereafter living in China for a while before coming to live in the United States in 2014.

Marlon L. Fick was born in Olathe, Kansas, in 1960. He is the author of *El niño de Safo* (Fuentes Mortera, 2000); *Selected Poems* (Fuentes Mortera, 2001); and *Histerias Minimas* (Fuentes Mortera, 2001); and the editor and translator of *The River Is Wide: 20 Mexican Poets* (University of New Mexico Press, 2005), for which he was named Best American Literary Translator by the Latitudes Foundation. He has received fellowships from the National Endowment for the Arts in Poetry in the U.S. and the ConaCulta in Mexico, and a Ramon Llull Award for Literature in Catalonia. His latest book is a novel, *The Nowhere Man* (Jaded Ibis Press, 2015). He is a senior lecturer in English at the University of Texas of the Permian Basin.

OTHER BOOKS FROM TUPELO PRESS

Silver Road: Essays, Maps & Calligraphies (hybrid memoir), Kazim Ali
Another English: Anglophone Poems from Around the World (anthology), edited by Catherine
  Barnett and Tiphanie Yanique
Personal Science (poems), Lillian-Yvonne Bertram
Everything Broken Up Dances (poems), James Byrne
Almost Human (poetry), Thomas Centolella
Land of Fire (poetry), Mario Chard
Hallowed (poems), Patricia Fargnoli
The Posthumous Affair (novel), James Friel
Poverty Creek Journal (memoir), Thomas Gardner
Leprosarium (poems), Lise Goett
My Immaculate Assassin (novel), David Huddle
Darktown Follies (poems), Amaud Jamaul Johnson
A God in the House: Poets Talk About Faith (interviews), edited by Ilya Kaminsky and
  Katherine Towler
Third Voice (poems), Ruth Ellen Kocher
The Cowherd's Son (poems), Rajiv Mohabir
Marvels of the Invisible (poems), Jenny Molberg
Lucky Fish (poems), Aimee Nezhukumatathil
The Life Beside This One (poems), Lawrence Raab
Intimate: An American Family Photo Album (hybrid memoir), Paisley Rekdal
Thrill-Bent (novel), Jan Richman
The Voice of That Singing (poems), Juliet Rodeman
Dirt Eaters (poems), Eliza Rotterman
Walking Backwards (poems), Lee Sharkey
Good Bones (poems), Maggie Smith
Swallowing the Sea (essays), Lee Upton
feast gently (poems), G. C. Waldrep
Legends of the Slow Explosion (essays), Baron Wormser
Ordinary Misfortunes (poetry), Emily Jungmin Yoon

See our complete list at www.tupelopress.org